A HISTORY OF LINCOLNSHIRE

Crowland drainage mills, 1807

THE DARWEN COUNTY HISTORY SERIES

A History of Lincolnshire

ALAN ROGERS

Drawings by Jim Laverty *and* Keith Woodcock

Cartography by Derek McFeeley

PHILLIMORE

1985

Published by
PHILLIMORE & CO. LTD.
Shopwyke Hall, Chichester, Sussex

ISBN 0 85033 546 9

Printed in Great Britain at the
University Press, Oxford

Contents

For Kathy, who was born there

List of Plates

The author is grateful for permission to reproduce the following plates: David Kaye: 4, 6, 12, 15, 21, 25, 26, 28, 32, 39, 41, 42, 43, 44, 47, 48; University of Cambridge Aerial Photographic Collection: 7, 9; Lincolnshire Library Services: 10, 35; *Lincolnshire Life*: 11; C.V. Middleton & Sons and City of Lincoln: 16; David Robinson: 17, 18, 33; Lawrence Elvin: 24; Grimsby Borough Council: 34; Humberside County Leisure Service: 38; *Lincolnshire Free Press and Spalding Guardian*: 49.

List of Maps

Preface

Faced with the request to up-date the first edition of *A History of Lincolnshire*, and mindful of all the work done on the county's history since 1969, especially by the History of Lincolnshire Committee (of which I was chairman from 1965 to 1979) and the various authors commissioned by that committee, as well as by other writers in books and journals, it seemed easiest to use the 1969 text as a basis and rewrite each chapter completely. This is what I have done; the text is now twice as long and (I hope) takes cognizance of the latest work done on Lincolnshire. Two new chapters have been added, and several of the earlier ones have been amalgamated.

Like the 1969 volume, this is still an interim report on the county's history. There is much we do not know about the past of this region. The History of Lincolnshire Committee (under its present chairman, Dr. Dennis Mills) has continued to publish regularly and it can confidently look forward to producing the last volumes of the series in the next four or five years. And even with this series complete, much more research is needed. Perhaps this book will provoke some authors to test its over-generalised conclusions.

I must thank many helpers with this revised edition. Professor Kathleen Major and Katherine Dixon amongst others gave me many comments on the earlier book. The Archives Office at Lincoln and its staff continue to offer help freely and willingly. David Robinson has commented on the text and made a number of valuable suggestions, expecially about the physical setting and drainage. Mrs. Myra Gough of Magee University College typed the text more than once with her accustomed efficiency and cheerfulness. But my main thanks must go to David Kaye of Louth. He has read the whole of this draft and offered many helpful comments; he has helped to compile the list of illustrations and found many of them. I am particularly grateful to him for all the hard work he has done for me.

Alan Rogers
Londonderry, June 1985

I Setting

The land of Lincolnshire lies trapped between the great rivers of Trent and Humber on the north west and north, the sea on the east and the Wash with its major rivers the Ouse and the Nene to the south; only in the south west is the county open to the rest of England. And this fact means that, despite the variations within the area which have left their mark on its political history, social structure and farming practices so that even today a 'woldsman' is seen to be a person apart from a 'fensman', there is an essential unity to the region which found expression from early times.

With some 72 miles from north to south and at its widest 55 miles from east to west, it is the second largest of all the English counties. It is nearly as far from the Humber to Stamford as from Stamford to London, nearly as far from the coast to the Trent as from the Trent to Cheshire. And within this large area there is a wide range of scenery and geographical features. There are hills and valleys, steep inland cliffs and undulating plateaux, wet fens and dry scrubby heathlands, limestone moors and sandy warrens, chalk plains and heavy clay basins, light gravelly loams and thick silts – hard rocks fit for building and soft soils ideal for farming.

Most people are convinced that Lincolnshire is flat. Even drivers along the Great North Road over the rolling heathlands of west Kesteven between Stamford and Newark still assume that Lincolnshire and the Fens are different terms for the same area, while the hundreds of people who holiday every year on the Lincolnshire coast firmly hold this opinion despite the fact that the main routes to Skegness and Mablethorpe cross the limestone uplands and pass over the southern Wolds.

One reason for the prevalence of this view may be that some of the different regions within the county merge into one another. There are some sharply defined features: the steep face of the Lincoln Cliff, the western edge of the northern Wolds and the even more abrupt former sea-cliffs on the southern Wolds. But elsewhere one passes without noticing from one region to another – from the limestone into the Witham Vale east of Lincoln for instance.

Boundaries

This is particularly true of the southern and western boundaries of the county. Along the south the river Welland provides part of the frontier, but a more or less artificial line across the Fens defines the rest.

11

In the south west, there is no clear dividing line between Lincolnshire and its neighbours; the county boundary divides almost identical villages, placing some in Lincolnshire and others in Rutland, Leicestershire or (further north) Nottinghamshire. North of Grantham the line joins the river Witham briefly before cutting across to the Trent.

Here at last is a major natural barrier. But the county boundary does not stay for long with the river. Just before it flows into the Humber, the Trent passes through a large flood plain, and part of this clay basin now lies in Lincolnshire. The Isle of Axholme, as it is called, together with the Yorkshire part of the Humberhead Marshes, Hatfield Chase, has its own characteristic countryside and its own settlement pattern.

The boundaries of Lincolnshire on the south and west are probably late in creation, relying for their delineation more on agreement between neighbouring communities over the use of tracts of common land or upon the boundaries of different estates than on natural features. But elsewhere there are natural frontiers. The Humber in the north provides a real barrier only partly lessened today by the new Humber bridge; the crossing of this treacherous water by ferry in earlier days was very hazardous.

To the east lies the coast. The shore line has fluctuated greatly over the ages. At one time it lay further to the east, bordered by chalk cliffs. Flooding, caused by the tilting of the land, the rise in sea level and climatic variations, at one time brought the coastline in successive waves further west until it reached to the eastern margin of the Wolds and up the Witham, Welland and Trent valleys. Today, along much of its length there are wide and once inhospitable marshes broken by a number of small rivers. On the central section for about 18 miles from Mablethorpe to Skegness, large dunes have been washed away in great floods as the former protecting shoals off-shore finally disappeared below sea level. The eroded material has been moved southwards into the Wash, that vast (and formerly more extensive) basin into which the Witham, Welland, Nene and Ouse all poured their waters like a huge sedimentation tank. The coastal marshes and fens of Lincolnshire despite periodic flooding have provided both a rich living for its inhabitants and a series of landing sites and havens for sea-goers.

These fluctuations and their consequent modifications of landscape and vegetation have constantly altered the face of the region. And Lincolnshire is still changing today, with both short-term man-made alterations and longer-term natural changes. It is a living land where men and the forces of nature meet face to face.

Regions

The most notable features of the map of Lincolnshire are the two areas of uplands, the limestone heathlands in the west and the chalk wolds in the east, with the vale between them. These mark off the major geographical and settlement regions of the county.

Of the lowlands, the largest is the Fens in the south east. Lincolnshire

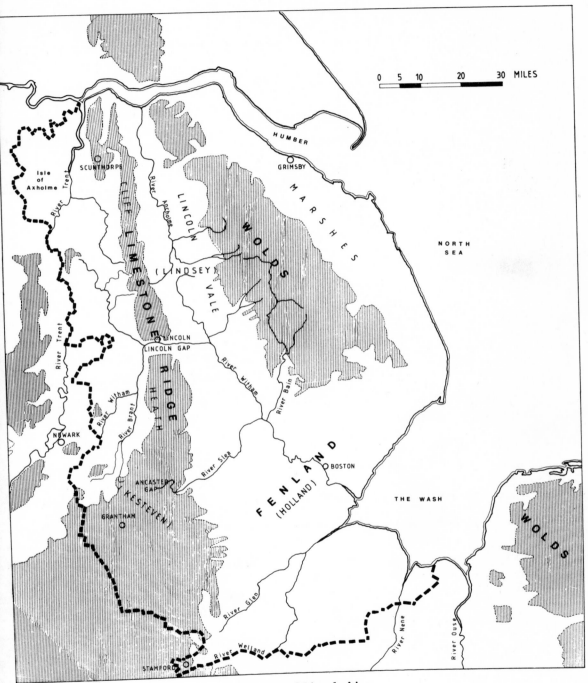

1. Regions of Lincolnshire.

13

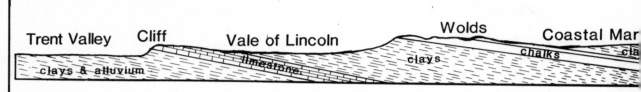

SECTION ACROSS NORTH LINCOLNSHIRE

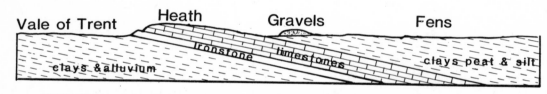

SECTION ACROSS SOUTH LINCOLNSHIRE (north of Grantham)

2. Sections across Lincolnshire (not to scale).

contains about one third of the great fenland region of England; the rest lies in Norfolk and Cambridgeshire. This is a complex area, divided between the silt fens and the peat fens. Although they have much in common with each other, the other lowland zones are all distinctive. The Marsh to the east of the Wolds, some 40 miles long and five to ten miles wide, runs northwards into Yorkshire; it is drained by short stubby streams which flow off the Wolds into the sea, and defended from salt-water invasion by sea walls which often form the platforms for sharply winding roads. The wet clay Lincoln Vale between the Wolds and the

14

heath, full of low hills sometimes with caps of sand or gravel, proved in earlier times to be a barrier to movement from the limestone uplands to the chalk uplands and the coast; its main line of communication was north-south. The Trent valley to the west of the limestone, with its loam and gravels, was fertile: river silt, boulder clay and patches of well-drained soils led to heavy settlement and intensive farming. Not so the small Isle of Axholme, some 10 by 15 miles in extent. Here early forests and later peat and large areas of freshwater flooding created by the congruence of three major river systems produced one of the most intractable landscapes in England; cut off from the rest of Lincolnshire by the Trent and from the rest of Yorkshire and Nottinghamshire by deep marshes, Axholme for long preserved an independent identity.

The uplands though relatively slight are distinctive. The Lincolnshire Wolds are part of a chalk belt stretching from Yorkshire into Norfolk, broken by the Humber and the rivers of the Wash. These rolling hills and downs, 45 miles long and rising to about 500 feet (Normanby le Wold), have their own particular scenery and settlement patterns; with deep valleys (especially in the southern half) and woodlands, they harbour some of the richest farms and estates in the county. The general north-south thrust of this ridge is confirmed by the early main roads along the length of the Wolds, but there is a marked difference between the north and south Wolds, divided roughly by a line from Market Rasen to Louth.

The other upland region is the limestone ridge. The tail end of that belt which sweeps across England in a curve from the Cotswolds through Oxfordshire, Northamptonshire, Leicestershire and Lincolnshire to the Humber. In Lincolnshire the region is divided into two. The Kesteven uplands south of the Lincoln Gap were noted for their rich soils and 'better air', but the Cliff to the north of Lincoln was poorer. The belt narrows as it goes northwards; about 20 miles wide when it enters the county, it only averages five to six miles just south of Lincoln, and from Lincoln to the Humber only two to three miles. It rises to 200-300 feet in parts of Kesteven where it is deeply cut by river basins. Along the western edge of this ridge are beds of ironstone, the reason for the later growth of the steel towns of Corby (Northants) and Scunthorpe; one of these beds forms a lesser ridge most clearly seen along the scarp between Lincoln and Grantham. On the eastern side of the heathland is a line of low clay hills capped and surrounded by gravels and watered by springs. The earliest and densest settlement in the county was along the edges of these uplands and in the valleys of the south, while the main routes through the region ran along the more barren top.

Routes and Rivers

The limestone ridge provided the county with its main overland link with the rest of England. But the water routes probably counted for more in Lincolnshire's story. The small but important havens on the coast like Tetney, Saltfleet and Wainfleet gave access to the rest of

15

eastern England and to the continent, while the mouths of the Humber-Trent and Wash, although dangerous, were the main points of entry. In the south the Nene and the Ouse drew upon a vast hinterland and built up foreign links, and the smaller rivers, the Welland, its tributaries the East and West Glen (sometimes known as the Eden and the Glen) and the Gwash fall off the limestone and drain across the southernmost parts of the county.

The land between the Wolds and the limestone uplands is drained in part by the Witham, a large river which flows south east from Lincoln to Boston and the Wash, assisted by the Slea flowing from the limestone (the Ancaster Gap) on the west and by the Bain flowing from the chalk

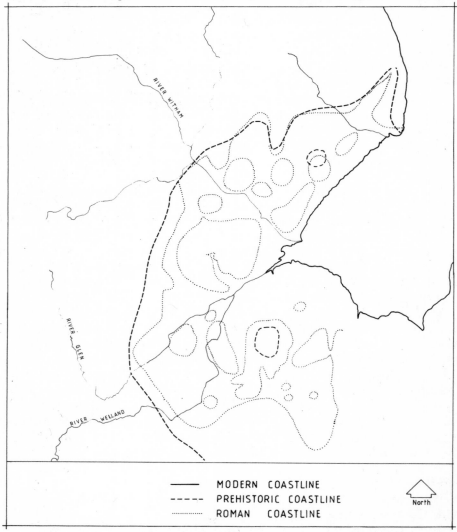

	MODERN COASTLINE
	PREHISTORIC COASTLINE
	ROMAN COASTLINE

North

3. Changes in the Lincolnshire coastline.

16

1. Cropmarks showing prehistoric barrow sites in the Welland valley. Other features can also be seen, including what is probably a pre-Roman farm site.

2. Bronze Age urn, found at Salmonby.

3. The Guthlac inscribed stone at Brotherhouse Bar, near Crowland.

4. Roman arch; Newport gateway, Lincoln.

5. Roman mosaic pavement, from the Winterton villa site.

6. Stow Church is on one of the early minster sites; the present building is mostly post-Conquest, but it retains some Anglo-Saxon features.

7. Site of a deserted medieval village: Brackenborough.

8. The impressive ruins of Crowland Abbey.

9. The site of Thornton Abbey from the air.

and sandstones of the southern Wolds on the east. The more northerly part of this vale contains the Ancholme which runs northwards into the Humber. To the west of the limestone the Trent flows northwards and empties into the Humber, bringing the life of the southern Pennines and the Midland plain into and through this region. The southerly part of the Trent-Belvoir valley carries the northward-flowing upper Witham and Brant rivers which, once they have joined, turn eastwards through the Lincoln Gap. The main thrust of the river system, like the upland areas, is from south to north.

The making of Lincolnshire

Once the basic material of the landscape had been laid down by successive waves of sedimentation, layer upon layer of soft and hard rocks, two main forces helped to make Lincolnshire look as it does today. First the land has tilted eastward and on several occasions sunk below sea-level. The erosion which followed created the scarp face which the limestone ridge presents to the west and the more gradual slope eastwards. The same pattern is true of the chalk Wolds deposited by the sea on top of a belt of sandstone, part of which can be seen in the Spilsby area. In places (as at West Keal) the sea has cut the east face of the chalk into cliffs.

The second major force was glaciation. The first Ice Age affected the whole county, smoothing the uplands and deepening the clay vale and fenland basin. In particular, it changed the course of the rivers. Originally, these followed the slope of the land eastwards from the lower Trent basin through the Ancaster Gap, the Lincoln Gap and the Humber Gap to the North Sea. But as the ice melted, the Trent turned northwards to flow into the Humber, and the upper Witham and Glen valleys developed as ice-edge meltwater channels. The various tributaries to the west of the limestone were gathered up by the Trent or the Witham so that today the Ancaster Gap is almost dry, an important area for naturalists as well as for historians. Only the Welland and the Gwash escaped this re-orientation, but their tributaries flow southwards for long distances before turning east.

The melting glaciers filled the valleys and covered the marshlands and much of the southern limestone with a patchy veneer of boulder clay on which heavy forests grew. Ridges and small islands of sand and gravel were left along the edges of the uplands and on the top of hills of clay. In the last glaciation, the ice only reached as far as the southern Wolds; a huge lake was created in the fenland basin, central Lincolnshire and lower Trent vale into which were deposited further extensive spreads of sand and gravel which were exposed when the ice melted. It was this pattern of river and soil which more than anything else affected where man lived and what he did in Lincolnshire, and the exposure of the different rocks and soils provided the region with its chalk, ironstone and limestone quarries and its sand and marl pits.

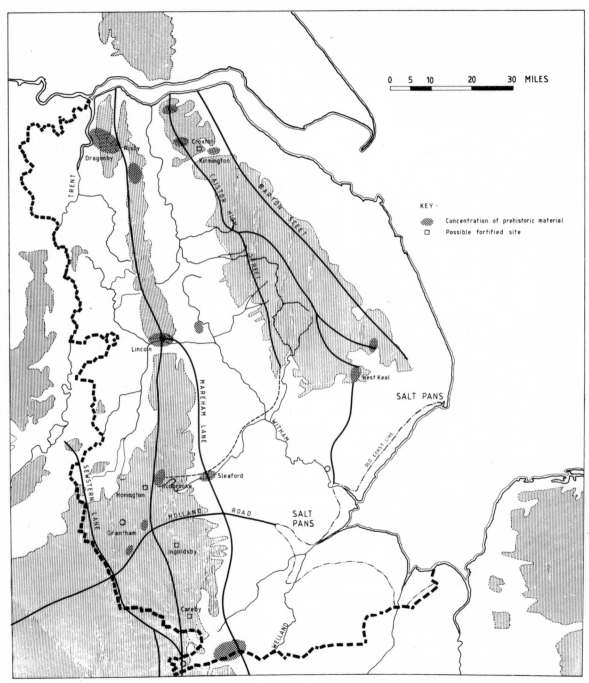

4. Prehistoric Lincolnshire.

II Prehistory

The earliest history of settlement in Lincolnshire is obscure for several reasons. The frequent flooding, drainage and intensive cultivation of the land mean that many early sites and objects either have been destroyed or are buried so deep under silt and peat that they are irrecoverable. Until the recent advent of aerial photography,there has been no systematic exploration of the county's archaeology, and the historian thus has to rely on chance finds which give only a partial picture of the life of early man in the region; they do not necessarily show where he lived though they may show where he was active.

Since the soils of large parts of the area which is now Lincolnshire were very suitable for early settlers, there can be little doubt that some areas were relatively heavily settled, though the evidence is at present thin. But even so, it is unlikely that the population of the region was very numerous until about 500 years before the Romans came. A few large families or clans roaming the fens and forests over long periods could account for all the Stone Age finds from the county. Occupation sites began in the late Neolithic and early Bronze periods. A major resettlement by local migration from the uplands to the valleys in the late Bronze Age, spread over several hundreds of years and apparently due more to climatic and associated vegetation changes than to successive waves of invaders, is the best interpretation of the materials from this period; for archaeologists today tend to stress continuity of occupation rather than conquest and dispossession. In the Iron Age, too, it may have been that the threat and fear of invasion rather than invasion itself brought about significant cultural and social changes; but one of the few facts that most archaeologists are agreed upon is that the population of this region apparently increased rapidly from about 500 B.C.

Travel and communications

More people travelled through the region than settled here in the centuries before the coming of the Romans. The geography of the area encouraged early man to pass through rather than occupy the land, and during most of the prehistoric period the parts to the east of the limestone belt remained something of a backwater, culturally well behind the rest of the county. In the very earliest phases, when what is now the North Sea was a rich plain, Lincolnshire comprised an area of foothills giving access to the higher land further to the west, and the earliest explorers may have passed through on foot from east to west; but when later the

19

sea flooded in and created the North Sea, the shape of the coastline despite some useful landing points encouraged those who now came by water to by-pass the region either to the north via the Humber, Ouse and Trent or to the south via the Wash, Welland, Nene and Ouse.

The overland routes of prehistoric Britain also tended to take early man through the region rather than persuade him to settle in it. Along the top of the limestone belt lay the great trackway (the Jurassic ridgeway) which ran from the south west of Britain into Yorkshire; it entered Lincolnshire at or near Stamford, ran over the uplands between the river courses to Coldharbour near Grantham, to Honington and along the scarp to Lincoln. A secondary route (Mareham Lane) followed the eastern edge of the limestone (probably for much of the time the coastline) to the Lincoln Gap where it joined the other road. From there the route lay north along the Cliff edge (Pottergate) to an early ferry on the Humber. This seems to have been the main route into the north, for the Trent and the Humberhead Marshes blocked access from other directions into the fertile lands of south Yorkshire.

Other prehistoric routes are known in the county. One (Sewstern Lane) ran from East Anglia and the Welland valley to the Trent near Newark, another (Salters Way) from the coast over the heathlands south of Grantham (Saltersford and Saltby) and into the Midlands. On the Wolds, High Street passed along the western edge from the Humber at South Ferriby to near Horncastle, and Barton Street ran along the eastern side from Barton to near Burgh le Marsh. Linking roads between High Street and Barton Street across the southern Wolds (the Bluestone Heath Road) and between Mareham Lane and the Jurassic Way across the Heath can be traced, and there are signs of connections between the Wolds and the limestone belt, along the river Bain at the southern end of the Wolds to the Witham and thence via Billinghay and Ruskington to the Ancaster Gap, and secondly a shorter and probably later route from the Wolds via Langworth to the Lincoln Gap. But some of these routes were used by the Romans and their prehistoric origins are not certain.

Hunting and gathering

Men probably first came to Lincolnshire in the inter-glacial periods as seasonal visitors, roaming in small groups hunting, fishing and gathering food, cutting wood, scraping skins and living rough. They moved over the low-lying land, as we see from the Kirmington flint tools dating from perhaps 250,000 B.C. (though these and other finds may have been carried some distance by later glaciations); later they were confined to higher ground by flooding and by the huge inland sea created by the melting glaciers – their flakes and hand axes are to be found in what were then woodland areas. Such conditions lasted for hundreds of years; between about 150,000 and 50,000 B.C., hunters and explorers from the Cresswell Crag caves in Derbyshire some 35 miles away entered the region.

After the last of the major glacial periods (c70,000 – 10,000 B.C.) which created the landscape and river systems into what broadly speaking we see today, man re-appeared about 8500 B.C. in a countryside which gradually grew more luxuriant as the climate grew warmer. Middle Stone Age hunters chased reindeer and bison through the tundra, and later assisted by dogs followed deer, oxen, pigs and horses in a woodland that changed from birch, hazel and pine to heavy forests of oak, elm and lime. Britain was joined to the continent at this time so that the migrant population probably came on foot moving from the rich low-lying plains to the east of Lincolnshire into the higher lands; the region was the very limit of human settlement.

A few sites were occupied, mostly on small west-facing pockets of sandy soil in the Scunthorpe area (Risby Warren and Sheffield Hill), and in the lower Trent valley (Willoughton), around Grantham, in the Ancaster Gap (Sudbrooke) and on the south and west slopes of the Wolds (Hall Hill, West Keal). The rich glacial soils of new boulder clay were apparently still not exploited for farming, and typical finds from this period are flints for arrows and spears, knives and scrapers, axes and picks; some of these may have been produced in large numbers for trade.

The first farms

The date of the earliest farming communities in Lincolnshire is disputed; sometime between 4000 and 3000 B.C. would seem to be about right. The settlements, located now mainly on the boulder clay, were pastoral with sheep, goats, pigs and cattle, rather than arable. The melting of the ice and the rise in sea-level which separated Britain from the continent may have made many areas too wet for cultivation. The distribution of sites suggests that these farmers entered the region from the south west along the Jurassic Way. Some of them passed to the Wolds along the rivers Slea and Bain; the 15 or so long barrows on the Wolds were probably built by these people; Giants Hill at Skendleby, the only one excavated, was found to contain eight burials dating from about 3500-2700 B.C.

Their farms seem to have been on lower ground than their burials. One or two larger and more settled communities are known in north west Lincolnshire (Dragonby) and in the Welland valley in the south. So far few finds have been located in the Fens but this may be because their farmsteads and burial places have been overlaid by peat and silt. Sites in the Welland valley are only now being revealed by aerial photography, and the number of finds from the cleared forest areas of the lower Trent valley and in the Lincoln Vale suggests that there may have been more Neolithic occupation in the fenland areas than we have evidence for at present. The finds from this first period of settled farmers include rough pottery, with flared-rim bowls and round-bottomed pots being particularly distinctive. Stone implements were apparently imported, flints from Norfolk and polished stone tools from Cumberland

Bronze Age pottery

and west Wales. The area no longer lay on the edge of human settlement; the frontier was further west and north.

The first metalworkers

About 2000 B.C. Britain attracted heavy settlements of people known to archaeologists as Beaker Folk. Although formerly felt to be aggressive warriors and conquerors, it is now thought likely that the progression from New Stone Age to Bronze Age was more peaceful and characterised by continuity rather than dispossession. Their fine red-clay pots with thin walls and flat bottoms, often decorated and sometimes with handles suggesting that they were used for drinking, are accompanied by many other objects, and the next 600 or so years may have seen groups of people living alongside each other with a wide range of different cultures, classes and religious and burial customs.

These settlers seem to have come into the area via the Humber and the rivers of the Wash (especially the Witham, the Bain and perhaps the Slea). They probably left many of the round barrows found on the Wolds, in the Marsh and along the eastern edge of the limestone uplands. Few of these survive intact after centuries of intensive farming, and some that are confidently ascribed to the Bronze Age may be later mounds (mills, gallows etc). Several have been excavated; some were re-used for later burials. 'Flat cemeteries' containing both inhumation and cremation burials are known as well as groups of barrows. The most important sites so far are at Stroxton, Little Gonerby and Long Bennington near Grantham, Broughton near Scunthorpe, Thoresway on the north Wolds, Bully Hills at Hougham by Louth, the 'Butterbump' near Skegness and Tallington in the Welland valley.

Occupation sites are less well known. The land was seemingly sinking once more and low-lying areas were being flooded. It may be that most of the new people by-passed the wetter lands for Yorkshire or the Midland plain. Those who settled chose sandy soils and gravels as in north west Lincolnshire (Risby Warren and Dragonby), the southern Wolds and the Ancaster Gap; but near Grantham sites on the limestone and ironstone are known as well.

Stone implements continued to be owned by these metal users – flint daggers, polished knives and even a flint sickle; and their pottery included large so-called 'bucket urns'. But the distinctive feature of this period is the metal work. Ornaments and weapons (probably ceremonial) were being made in copper and gold before 2000 B.C. but these metals were quickly supplemented by bronze. The range of bronze objects from Lincolnshire is wide – awls, knives, daggers (one from a barrow with a whetstone), razors, axes and ear-rings. As time went on, palstaves, spearheads and rapiers appeared in place of daggers. Gold ornaments include an armlet from Cuxwold in the north Wolds and a torc from near Haxey. A hoard from Appleby near Scunthorpe contained bronze objects which were apparently deliberately broken; it may have been buried as a votive or ritual deposit.

22

The later Bronze Age

From about 1300 to 600 B.C. a further change in climate and vegetation took place; the warm dry Continental weather gave way to the cooler, wetter Oceanic. This was when much of the Lincolnshire peat was laid down; the forests of Axholme for instance became a bog. But the chalk and limestone uplands seem to have been largely abandoned in favour of well-drained river valleys – especially the Welland and the Trent and some of the clay valleys of the limestone belt. Finds from the Fens seem to indicate some settlement there, and the southern Wolds saw some late Bronze Age occupation with perhaps continuity from earlier periods. The heaviest concentration still lay in the north west, with another cluster near the Lincoln Gap. Most of the evidence however consists of chance finds; settlement sites are still rare although one may lie at Washingborough and another at Brigg.

The metalwork of these people was of a high order. At first objects were imported but some native metal-working can be adduced. New stronger materials were introduced and it became possible to work in sheet metal – swords and spears with leaf-shaped blades, socketed axes and buckets are known. Some were of high quality like the Witham sword and the Billinghay sword and shields; these river finds may have been votive offerings. Hoards have been found at Caythorpe, West Halton and Burton on Stather close to the route into Yorkshire where population was apparently increasing at this time. The Lincolnshire region lay at the northern edge of Britain's metal-working area; these hoards may thus be associated with trade, but at least one, Nettleham near Lincoln, seems to be connected with a local metal-working industry.

The discovery of a number of dug-out canoes, a coracle at South Ferriby and a plank-built boat at Brigg, indicates some river-borne traffic and/or ferry services. Many come from the lower Witham between Lincoln and Tattershall but others have been found on the Ancholme, the lower stretches of the Trent and the Welland at Deeping.

The Iron Age

Bronze Age cultures persisted in parts of the area alongside the newer cultures of the Iron Age down to the coming of the Romans. Although Lincolnshire has not yet produced clear signs of a heavy Iron Age occupation, there is enough to indicate that the newer cultural waves of the period 500 to 120 B.C. had their impact on the region. Iron Age Lincolnshire formed part of a wider territory stretching from Yorkshire to the Thames, bound together by trade and exchange and by new traditions of burial, pottery making, metalwork and decoration.

Finds of the earliest Iron Age farmers are many but settlement sites are rare. Few inhumation cemeteries have been discovered. Much of the evidence comes from the south of the county, along the limestone belt and from the north west, but there are also signs of farming in the Fens and Marsh and of salt-making on the coast. An occupation site in the

Ancaster Gap showed signs of arable farming (wheat and barley), stock rearing (cattle, pigs and sheep), domestic animals (horses and dogs), residence (pits, pottery, horn fragments and brooches) and domestic activities such as grinding and weaving (querns, loom weights and spindle whorls). Fragments of ornaments and (again seemingly ceremonial) swords, scabbards and shields have been dredged from the Trent, and the famous bronze shield and the bronze trumpet from the Witham near Tattershall indicate that individuals or groups of taste, wealth and power lived in the locality. The Ancaster Gap site was apparently more of a peasant farmstead or hamlet, although not all the area has been excavated; but nearby the hill fort at Honington, guarding the Jurassic Way at its crossing of the Ancaster Gap, reveals powerful organisation and sophistication in this region. Yarborough Camp at Kirmington is another Iron Age hill fort, and Round Hills Ingoldsby and Careby Camp are possible examples.

Later in the Iron Age signs of the people usually recognised as Celts appear in coins and trade objects similar to those from all over the south east of Britain. High quality metal work in bronze, gold and silver, much of it with parallels on the continent, reveals the presence of skilled armourers and master craftsmen and a rich noble class which patronised them. The harness pieces from Ulceby are particularly fine and suggest, if not the use of chariots, at least the ceremonial use of horses.

Settlement sites from the late Iron Age (c. 150 -45 B.C.) are more plentiful and some continued in occupation into the Roman period. They are dense in the Grantham area (Colsterworth, Ancaster and Old Sleaford), at the north end of the Wolds (South Ferriby with its coin hoard, Kirmington and Dragonby) and in the Welland valley (Tallington), but other areas await investigation. Some of the material suggests that a number of settlers entered the region direct from the continent instead of passing through south east England and moving north. Coarse handmade pottery existed alongside fine wheelmade wares, some of them imported, and pins and buckets throw light on the way of life of these people, querns on their farming.

The Lincolnshire region became notable for the wide range and high quality of its metal work, and some of its products were exported to other parts of Britain. The use of animal motifs, especially heads (as in the Kirmington spout) in brooches and other bronze ornaments, was particularly characteristic. There was some decline in this advanced metal art in the last years of the Iron Age.

The history of this region in the years immediately before the coming of the Romans is obscure. Only one fort from this period is known for sure, Colsterworth in the south west, a later Roman posting town. The area shows signs of outside influence; some continental coins were in use (Grimsby and Sleaford), and coins of the Brigantes north of the Humber, of the Coritani of Leicestershire and of the Catuvellauni to the south have been found in the region. Although there is little evidence of Belgic settlement in Lincolnshire, the sites at Ancaster, Old Sleaford (perhaps

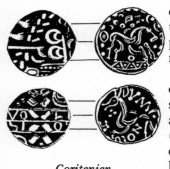

*Coritanian
coins*

24

a provincial centre; they were certainly minting coins there before the Romans came) and Dragonby suggest the presence of new settlers. It may be that Lincolnshire was at that time what it was after the Romans left, a territory disputed between larger neighbouring powers. On the whole the Coritani prevailed; by the first century B.C. they seem to have welded the various elements of a wide region covering north Northamptonshire, Leicestershire, parts of Nottinghamshire and parts of Lincolnshire into a complex group under a rule based on Leicester and perhaps other more local centres such as Lincoln; their area of influence extended up to the Humber though it may have excluded the Wolds where there are indications of people related to the Celtic tribe of the Parisi from Yorkshire. By the time the Romans came, almost the whole area of Lincolnshire seems to have been under the control of the Coritani.

Witham shield

III The Romans

Of the tribes which surrounded the territory of Lincolnshire when the Romans landed in south east Britain, the Catuvellauni to the south were amongst the first to submit to the invaders at Colchester in A.D. 43. The Iceni of East Anglia resisted fiercely, as did the Brigantes to the north. The Coritani offered little resistance and their lands were occupied early, their rulers retained as 'client' kings by the Romans. The area of Lincolnshire soon saw the Ninth Legion moving northwards from Colchester to a major fortification at Newton on Trent; the invading army seems to have entered the county roughly along the lines of the Jurassic ridgeway and Mareham Lane. Camps were established at Great Casterton, perhaps at Colsterworth or Easton and at Ancaster; a first camp may also have been built at Lincoln, either to the south or north of the Gap.

The first frontier

The troops halted behind the rivers Trent and Severn to consolidate their gains, and for a time the region formed part of the frontier of the Empire. Forts were built at regular intervals along Ermine Street – Saltersford and Navenby in addition to those established during the invasion. In A.D. 47 the great Fosse Way was laid out with a legionary fortress at Lincoln and a series of forts on or close to the line of the road; the most important of these forts, Margidunum and Thorpe, lie just over the present county boundary. The line was continued from Lincoln northwards, with roadside settlements at regular intervals at Owmby and Hibaldstow, to Old Winteringham on the Humber. It was a frontier which could be supplied by both road and water via the Trent, Humber and Witham.

The revolt of the Iceni under Boudicca in A.D. 61 was suppressed harshly, but by A.D. 71 when the invaders faced fresh threats north of the Humber it was possible for them to move the army from Lincoln to York. The Lincolnshire area ceased to be part of a military zone; instead it was administered from Romanised Leicester. Lincoln's brief life as a legionary fortress came to an end.

The Roman achievement

Roman Britain was occupied but not colonised: new technology (especially communications systems) and new administrative machinery and personnel were introduced, but native settlement patterns and customs were largely left unaltered. Indeed pockets of Iron Age culture seem to have persisted in the Wolds and the Welland valley. But few people can have been left completely untouched by the way of life which the Romans brought.

As elsewhere earlier tracks were converted into metalled roads. The Jurassic ridgeway became for much of its length a main through-route (Ermine Street), although in places abandoning the winding earlier corridor for a straight path across the heathlands somewhat to the east. Settlements grew up along its route to the Humber where a ferry was established at Winteringham-Brough. An offshoot from this road was built north westwards into Yorkshire (Tillbridge Lane), crossing the Trent at Littleborough. Mareham Lane south of Bourne became the Roman King Street with a link across the heath to Ermine Street at Ancaster; it continued north of Bourne to Old Sleaford and perhaps as far as Lincoln. A native track on the Wolds northwards from Burgh le Marsh was similarly metalled and an extension to the coast seems to have connected with a ferry across the Wash to the Norfolk coast. Other earlier tracks like Sewstern Lane were metalled in whole or in part.

Waterways formed part of the new and more efficient network throughout the region. Engineers constructed the Car Dyke, 56 miles long, linking the Nene near Peterborough to the Witham near Lincoln; it served as both a catchwater drain and a canal. The route to York was completed by joining the Witham to the Trent by means of the Fosse Dyke.

Roman statuette

Roman Lincolnshire

Romano-British sites of all periods are known in the county. The villa at Norton Disney dates from the first century while that at Great Casterton would not seem to be earlier than the fourth century. These sites are thickly located on the southern Wolds and along the edges of the limestone uplands, as at Denton in the west where there are also signs of Iron Age occupation and in the Bourne area in the east. The best known are Winterton and Horkstow with their fine mosaic pavements and bath-houses, but others are at Stoke Rochford, Haceby, Scampton and Roxby. Centres of settlement emerged, too small to be towns but larger than villas, like Stainfield and Sapperton on the road across the Heath or Ludford and Ulceby on the Wolds. Several of these lay over Iron Age sites and show signs of having progressed from one culture to the other as at Dragonby and Kirmington in the north or Foston near Grantham. Other sites have recently been excavated in south Lincolnshire (Whaplode, Holbeach and in the Welland valley). Roman coins at Iron Age hill forts (Yarborough and Honington) again suggest a process of assimilation.

The strength of Roman culture varied from settlement to settlement. Some seem to have been fully Romanised with buildings of an advanced style and imported luxury goods such as fine pottery and glass, while

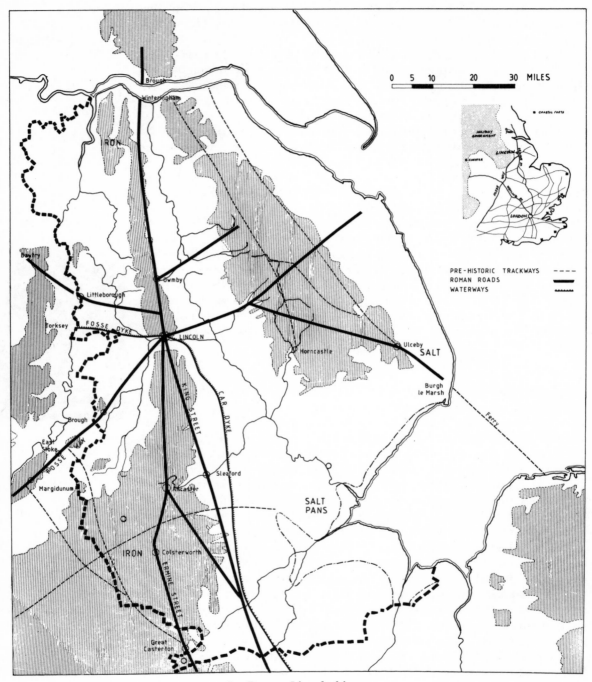

0   5   10   20   30 MILES

PRE-HISTORIC TRACKWAYS ----
ROMAN ROADS ━━━
WATERWAYS ～～～

Brough
Winteringham
IRON
Bawtry
Owmby
Littleborough
Torksey
FOSSE DYKE
LINCOLN
Horncastle
Ulceby
SALT
Burgh
le Marsh
Ferry
KING STREET
CAR DYKE
Brough
East
Stoke
FOSSE
Sleaford
Margidunum
Ancaster
SALT
PANS
IRON
Colsterworth
ERMINE STREET
Great
Casterton

COASTAL FORTS
MILITARY
GOVERNMENT
CHESTER
LINCOLN
LONDON

5. Roman Lincolnshire.

others were only lightly Romanised. The various religions of the Empire are represented by a few shrines and temple sites to Apollo, Mercury, Mars and other deities as well as to the Emperor. Some Celtic gods were 'Romanised' as can be seen from inscriptions at Nettleham and Ancaster, and a ritual gold 'crown' from Deeping St James may indicate a temple in that area. Christianity was introduced no later than the early third century; Lincoln seems to have had a bishop by A.D. 314 and an apparently Christian cemetery was in use at Ancaster by the fourth century.

Roman towns

More characteristic of the process of Romanisation was the emergence of towns. At Great Casterton, the early fort was abandoned and the civilian settlement which had grown up along the road to the west of it became the nucleus of a defended and wealthy town, while at Ancaster a town was built over the fort. On the Wolds Caistor which may have originated as a military outpost developed into a small walled town, while Horncastle also became a town, later walled. Sleaford situated where King Street crossed the Slea probably continued from the Iron Age as a larger settlement. Posting stations on the arterial roads (Great Casterton, Colsterworth, Ancaster, Hibaldstow) assisted the flow of traffic throughout the region.

Such places became centres for a way of life different from that pursued in the villages and farmsteads. The style and quality of the pottery and ornaments; the road systems inside the walls (irregular at Great Casterton, regular at Ancaster) and the extra-mural suburbs at Ancaster, Saltersford and Great Casterton; the temple sites and shrines at Ancaster, Dragonby, Kirmington and perhaps Caistor with its lead casket – all these reveal something of the Roman social and cultural way of life. Stone buildings as at Great Casterton with its bath-house, apparently a resting station for travelling officials, Ancaster and Saltersford, reflect wealth and influence. Cemeteries associated with towns have been found outside Great Casterton, Ancaster and Horncastle. Great Casterton, Sleaford and one or both of the Wold towns may have served as administrative centres for the area around, but there is no certain evidence for this.

Romano-British pottery

Lincoln

Lincoln was of course the main Roman town of the region. There are few signs of pre-Roman occupation on the site although it must have been an important crossing point on the Jurassic Way and it may have served as a regional centre for the Coritani. But the first major settlement was the Ninth Legion's fortress of some 41 acres on the hilltop to the north of the gap. Its strategic value, with steep slopes on three sides, enabled it to dominate a wide territory, overlooking the Wolds and controlling the land routes of Ermine Street and the Fosse Way; and it lay at the heart of the waterway network of the Car Dyke, Witham and Fosse Dyke. After the troops left, the town served as York's 'back-up' city.

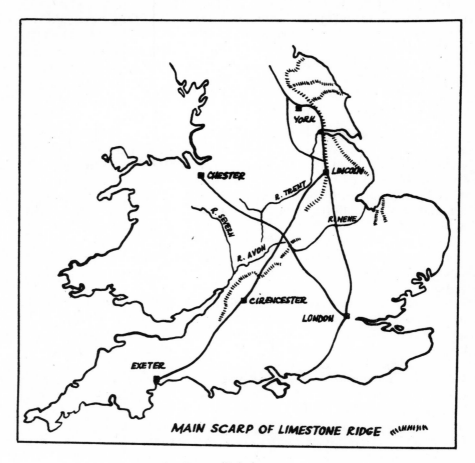

MAIN SCARP OF LIMESTONE RIDGE

6. Roman Britain.

From A.D. 77 Lincoln became one of four colonial centres in the province of Britain, a home for paid-off soldiers and officials with many of the amenities of a town nearer the centre of Roman civilisation. Stone walls and gates surrounded the civil town and by the early third century a further 56 acres down the steep slope to the south had been walled in. Fragments of the walls and gates survive in the castle walls, Newport Arch, Eastgate and elsewhere. Across the bottom of the gap a causeway was built, a flood relief system installed (the Sincil Dyke), and a suburb grew up on this newly drained land.

Although small (Verulamium had 200 acres and London 330) Lincoln had all the luxuries of a Roman city such as piped water, public cisterns and large buildings with central heating. There are relatively few signs of industry in Roman Lincoln although some pottery and brick kilns have been unearthed. This was no mere native capital upgraded; rather it was a new foundation, a planned city built to foreign standards. It directly administered its own territory, a large but as yet undetermined area to the north and east which became responsible for meeting the city's needs.

Newport arch, Lincoln

Exploitation

The Romans exploited the natural resources of the region. Iron was quarried and smelted in the Scunthorpe area and in the forests of the south west (Colsterworth, South Witham, Saltersford, Corby Glen, Pickworth etc). Stone was extracted at Barnack, Greetham near Lincoln, Ancaster and elsewhere. The county had its share of the pottery industry from the first to the fourth centuries; some of it was sold in market centres locally and some exported out of the region.

Above all, Lincolnshire's greatest asset, the land, was extensively used. Corn-drying kilns as at Great Casterton, Winterton and Sleaford are a sign of intensive farming. The coastal areas came under the heavy hand of the exploiter. After the inundations of the Bronze Age, the fens had been drying out. This may have been due to the development of a series of protective banks and shoals just off-shore, but the land was apparently some 15 feet higher than today with the coastline lying in parts further to the east. The area consisted of a number of islands in a sea of mud, and during the Iron Age settlement had been possible in these coastal lands and there had been salt-making near the shore. But it would seem that the region was first systematically developed by the Romans, perhaps under the direction of an Imperial department of state; indeed, the area may have been ceded to the Empire by the Iceni during the early years of the occupation. The cutting of the Car Dyke and the channelling of parts of the lower Witham (said to have been worshipped by the natives) may have been as much to drain the land as to make transport easier.

The coastal saltings continued to function until the end of the second century, and a number of pottery kilns have been found. But most of the evidence for the chief use of the land, arable and pastoral farming of an advanced type, has probably been obliterated by later flooding and intensive cultivation, though signs of roads and field systems are beginning to emerge as a result of detailed surveys. It is clear that this region, once thought to have been largely empty until the later drainage era, was heavily settled especially from about A.D. 120 to the late third century when flooding occurred once more. There was a short-lived revival of large-scale occupation in the fourth century but during this later phase some of the land seems to have been worked from estates situated on the edge of the fens and the limestone belt in the Bourne area.

The withdrawal of the Romans

The collapse of Roman rule in this region as elsewhere in Britain was gradual. In the late fourth century, in response to a series of concerted attacks on the frontiers of the Empire, a re-organisation of the province's administration took place. There is no clear evidence in Lincolnshire of the late Roman coastal defences known as the Saxon Shore, but one fort may have existed in the area of Burgh le Marsh. Horncastle and Caistor had walls built late in the Roman period, and there are signs of refortification at Great Casterton, Ancaster and even at Lincoln itself. In A.D. 407 the armies were withdrawn from Britain, and about 430 new mercenary troops came in; within 15 years, these Saxon *foederati* had revolted and other invaders made raids along the coast.

There is no evidence in Lincolnshire of any great disaster; perhaps the changeover was relatively peaceful. Although little is known of Lincoln between the fourth and seventh centuries, there are few signs of violent destruction and it is possible that the city was never completely deserted. Indeed there is some evidence that civic life continued or was soon resumed. At Great Casterton villa, signs of fire can be seen but it was not extensive, and the close association of Anglo-Saxon burials with Roman sites at Great Casterton, Ancaster, Sleaford and Caistor suggests peaceful infiltration rather than conquest.

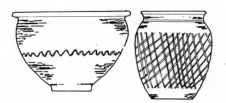

Romano-British pottery

IV Anglo-Saxons, Danes and Normans

The new arrivals from northern Germany and the Low Countries who entered the area in the fifth and sixth centuries found in the Wash and Humber estuaries reminiscent of their homeland coastlines; but the process of invasion and settlement is far from clear. When the region emerged from the obscurity of the migration period,it was divided into two parts. In the north was Lindsey, a small kingdom whose origin may even be pre-Saxon; its name indicates an early connection with Lincoln and there are signs of British survival in the names of its earliest kings. Lindsey had a considerable measure of organisation, based on Lincoln, Stow or some more rural centre;it had its own bishop recognised by 677 as independent of the neighbouring bishops of Northumbria (York) and Mercia (Lichfield).The southern half of the county formed part of the kingdom of the Middle Angles probably centred on Leicester; it too had its bishop. The Fens, inundated again during the fifth and sixth centuries, appear as a more or less untamed frontier land between the kingdoms of Lindsey, East Anglia and Middle Anglia.

Neither Lindsey nor Middle Anglia was large enough to survive in the troubled days of the Anglo-Saxon kingdoms, though Lindsey did better than most of the smaller kingdoms. The Middle Angles were absorbed by pagan Mercia which under Penda, one of its greatest kings, was waging war against the Christian British in the west and the Christian Northumbrians in the north and east. Some of his battles with the Northumbrians probably took place in Lindsey which changed hands between Mercian and Northumbrian overlords many times before Mercia established a predominance in 678. Throughout this time how-ever Lindsey preserved its own identity; it is mentioned as a separate political unit up to about 800, and the names of its kings were cherished for many centuries. It probably ceased to exist as an independent entity before the Danish invasions destroyed most of the remaining Anglo-Saxon kingdoms, but the struggle between Mercia and Northumbria for control over this area left its mark on the later history of the region in the separate identity of medieval Lindsey and in the quarrels between the bishops of Lincoln and the archbishops of York who claimed Lindsey as a part of the northern province of the Church.

*Statue of
Havelok
the Dane*

The Danes

The Danes began to make seasonal raids on the shrines and religious houses, the main centres of wealth and culture along the coast of

33

England, in the last years of the eighth and early ninth centuries; but when about 850 their aim changed from the gathering of plunder to permanent conquest, the Humber and its tributaries were once again an important point of entry for the invaders.

The main Danish attack was concentrated on the kingdoms of East Anglia and Northumbria. The Lincolnshire region was thus heavily involved. Danish armies passed between Yorkshire and East Anglia, destroying monasteries such as Bardney and Crowland and establishing temporary forts at Maxey, Gainsborough and elsewhere. From their winter headquarters at Torksey on the Trent, they launched an attack on Mercia in 874, set up a puppet king and established the territory known from their main strongholds as the land of the 'Five Boroughs'. Whether this territory covered the whole of the later Lincolnshire is not certain; in 886 when Alfred king of Wessex made the Treaty of Wedmore with the Danes of East Anglia recognising the southern Danelaw, it is not clear whether any part of the lands north of the Welland was included in that new unit.

Two of the Five Boroughs, Lincoln and Stamford, lay in the area which later became Lincolnshire. Almost nothing is known of Saxon Lincoln before the Danish conquests apart from the fact that Bede indicated that it had a 'prefect' in charge in 627, but the invaders quickly recognised its strategic value and although it was defended against the Danes they twice stormed and garrisoned it. Even less is known of Stamford, but under the Danes, like Lincoln, it engaged in minting, pottery making and trade with Scandinavia. All the Five Boroughs were fortified by the Danes and served as centres for the muster of troops. Thus when soon after the death of Alfred in 899 the conquest of Danish England began in earnest, particular attention was paid to these towns. In 917 Derby was captured by the English king and in the following year Leicester, Stamford and Nottingham fell. Within a short time Lincoln too had submitted.

The last conquests

For a time the Lincolnshire area lay on the frontier between the new kingdom of England and the new pagan Norse kingdom of York. War was endemic; in 940 the lands of the Five Boroughs were acknowledged as part of the kingdom of York, and Scandinavian sagas indicate that north Lincolnshire at least was regarded as being under the control of the York kings. Coin evidence suggests that this rule extended south to Stamford where a sub-king with his own currency may have been set up. But political domination over the area changed several times until in 954 the York king was killed in battle and the threat from the Norse at York was removed.

But Norsemen from overseas continued to harass the shores of England and Lincolnshire saw a good deal of the fighting. Gainsborough with its riverside camp became the headquarters for the conquest of England by

7. The Danelaw.

king Swein of Denmark and his sons in 1013-16, and it was there that Cnut was chosen to succeed his father as king of Denmark and England:

> After Swein's death, Cnut stayed with his host in Gainsborough . . . and an agreement was made between him and the people of Lindsey to supply him with horses and then set out together and harry. Then king Aethelred came

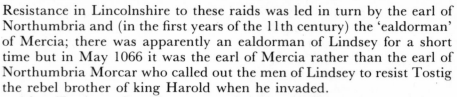

with levies at full strength into Lindsey before they were prepared, and they made raids and burned and slew every human being they could find.

Resistance in Lincolnshire to these raids was led in turn by the earl of Northumbria and (in the first years of the 11th century) the 'ealdorman' of Mercia; there was apparently an ealdorman of Lindsey for a short time but in May 1066 it was the earl of Mercia rather than the earl of Northumbria Morcar who called out the men of Lindsey to resist Tostig the rebel brother of king Harold when he invaded.

After Tostig, a Danish army under Harold Hardrada entered the Humber and moved into Yorkshire where Hardrada was killed at Stamford Bridge by Harold. Immediately after the battle news came of the invasion of William duke of Normandy and Harold hurried south, leaving the sheriff of Lindsey to restore order in the north. The Normans of course won at Hastings, and in 1068 William himself came north to suppress revolts. He entered Lincolnshire after ravaging Yorkshire but in general the county was peaceful. Although resistance smouldered north of the Humber and in the south where the dispossessed Hereward led a rising in the fens around Ely in 1070, the Norman occupation of Lincolnshire was not on the whole accompanied by violence.

Social fabric

Lincolnshire is a county of villages. They lie along the edges and in the valleys of the limestone belt, on the floors of the clay basins, throughout the marshlands and along the coast. There are scattered homesteads and areas of dispersed settlement in the fenlands and on the upper heaths and north Wolds, but even in these regions villages exist, often with quasi-urban characteristics because they serve a larger population in the area around. Places like Kirton, Pinchbeck, Billing-borough and Swineshead which elsewhere would be regarded as large villages have the feeling of small rural towns because of the range of services they offer.

Saxon coins

Many of these villages may have had a prehistoric origin even if they now possess an Anglo-Saxon or Danish name. Some continuity from Roman and pre-Roman periods is clear. The Anglo-Saxon principalities and the later county divisions may go back to pre-Roman groupings among the Coritani tribes, just as the name of Lincoln incorporates pre-Saxon elements. Village names like Walesby and Waltham indicate the survival of some 'Welsh' (Romano-British) peoples, and the element -scot in Scotter and Scotton – shows that the so-called Scottish peoples were also present; more of these people no doubt continued to live in the region under new landlords and hidden from view under new placenames.

The evidence then suggests that in Lincolnshire the Anglo-Saxon migrations in the fifth and sixth centuries were relatively peaceful. But it is well to remember that less is known about the history of these years than about any other period. Finds are few and difficult to interpret, and the study of placenames is not yet complete. Known occupation sites

36

are rare, probably because they lie under the present towns and villages of the county. Old Sleaford is thus important: the centre of settlement moved to the north and west of the early site, and excavations in the 1960s revealed a more or less unbroken sequence of occupation from the Iron Age through the Roman period into the early Anglo-Saxon years. Dragonby and Kirmington have not yet revealed such continuity and at Ancaster where once again pre-Roman, Roman and Anglo-Saxon material has been found, there are signs of a period of depopulation or migration to a new site nearby before the medieval village grew up on the earlier site. We do not know which pattern was the more common, continuous occupation or dispossession and settlement on new sites.

But on the whole the pattern of villages and towns of today reflects the handiwork of the Anglo-Saxons and their successors the Danes. Members of all the races which took part in the invasions, except the Jutes, apparently settled in Lincolnshire. There are signs of Saxons as early as about 450, and the Frisians left their mark in names like Frieston. But the majority of settlers were Angles. Some early cemeteries have been found, the most important being at Sleaford, Elkington in the Wolds and Loveden Hill north of Grantham containing pagan cremation and inhumation burials. The metalwork among the grave goods shows some influence of the earlier Celtic work for which the region is noted, perhaps another indication of the survival of Romano-British people.

After the conversion of the new settlers to Christianity, the archaeological material becomes less useful. The basic evidence for the history of the settlement consists of placenames and the pattern of villages. A large number of placenames end in -ingas, an Anglo-Saxon element made up from the name of people who settled there or variant forms of it, like the Deepings or Folkingham; although these may not represent the earliest waves of invasion as was once thought, they show the

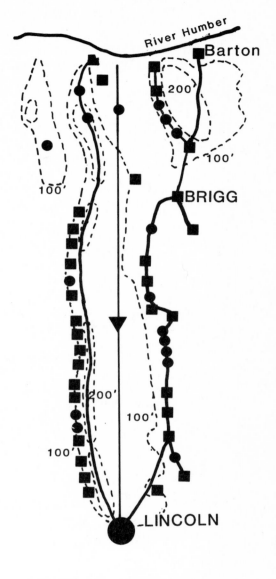

■ Villages with Saxon names
● Villages with Danish or Scandinavian names
▼ Spital-in-the-Street

8. Villages and roads of north Lincolnshire.

strength of Anglo-Saxon colonisation in the sixth century in this area. The settlers seem to have entered along the rivers Welland, Witham, Slea and Ancholme and then along the Roman roads, especially Ermine Street and King Street. A few of their villages lie in the Fens between Boston and Spalding but rather more cluster along both sides of the limestone heath; there are several on the Wolds.

The pattern created by these Anglo-Saxon colonists persists today. Villages lie on the springline along the edges of both the limestone and the chalk uplands where porous rocks overlie heavier clays. Such a location gave access to the areas of heath on the higher lands and to the meadows and pastures below. This pattern is most clearly seen just north of Lincoln. Here the Roman road runs directly northwards across the limestone belt, ignoring all settlements. A second road, one lane of the earlier prehistoric ridgeway, clings closer to the cliff edge and below it lie villages with early Anglo-Saxon names, Cammeringham, Fillingham, etc. So regular is the pattern that it has been suggested that this is an area of planned settlement, but this seems unlikely. Each village is connected to the cliff-top road by a lane running down the hillside and on into the low pastures. On the other side of the limestone belt lies a second north-south line of villages connected by a road which is clearly later, winding from village to village through the open fields.

9. Cross-section of Lincolnshire Cliff (not to scale).

Further south much the same pattern is visible. Along both edges of the limestone heath, villages grew up on the spring line. In the clays of the Witham, Belvoir and Trent valleys, a number of ridges and little hills capped with gravel provided dry sites for rows of villages such as Blankney and Billinghay or more isolated settlements like Bassingham. Along the eastern edge of the limestone facing the Fens were low islands of gravel, each of which attracted early occupation (Heckington,

38

Helpringham, Horbling, Billingborough). There was virtually no settlement on the limestone plateau and little on the top of the Wolds. The boulder clay edge of the Marsh received some early sites (Alvingham, Cockerington) but in general the marshlands were left until the pressure of population and the demand for land grew. Few settlements were made on the coastal silt belt or on islands in the Fens which were a home for refugees like St Guthlac at Crowland; flooding in this area in the fifth and sixth centuries seems to have deterred occupation though not, of course, exploitation.

Scandinavian in-filling

Between 600 and 800 population grew, more land was cultivated and new villages were formed, sometimes as subsidiary settlements from the main villages. In the low lands of the Trent valley west of the Cliff and in the forest areas of south Kesteven, sites which were occupied seasonally or occasionally – summer pastures, meadows, or forest clearances – became the homes of permanent settlements with names including *-ing*, *-feld* or *-ley*. The Danish incursions ranging over nearly a century added to this population. Although some historians have suggested that the conquest was not accompanied or followed by the settlement of large numbers of new inhabitants, that the armies were relatively small and that the intrusive cultural features of placenames, linguistic elements and customs were the result of conquest rather than colonisation, the signs of a substantial Danish immigration into Lincolnshire, the heaviest in England, seem unanswerable. More than 250 placenames ending in the Danish *-by* (village or homestead) are known, and 'hybrid' forms combining Anglo-Saxon and Danish elements are on the whole rare. Other characteristics of this region in the later Anglo-Saxon period suggest that we are here dealing with a folk movement, a migration of land-hungry people who settled side by side with the English rather than a conquering aristocracy ruling over a subject people. The routes followed seem to have been once more the rivers and the Roman roads. The Wolds show signs of heavy Danish occupation, especially in the Horncastle area, 'the most strongly Scandinavian part of Lincolnshire, and indeed of the whole Danelaw'. There were extensive settlements in south Kesteven, but the Fens were not densely occupied until later.

The original Danish settlement in small consolidated groups for military purposes expanded as the Scandinavian population grew rapidly. New villages were established, often on poorer soils. The pattern created by these later settlers is not always clear. In some areas, especially in the more congenial river valleys, they appear to have filled gaps with villages of their own; in other places they established hamlets in outlying parts of the lands belonging to the original settlement, often to be seen in the element *-thorpe*, a subordinate or secondary settlement, as at Thurlby by Bourne with its Northorpe, Southorpe and Obthorpe, or at West Ashby with Midthorpe and Farthorpe.

During the years before the Norman Conquest, a small Norse element

Anglo-Saxon pottery

39

(Normanby, Normanton) appeared among the settlers. But the coming of the Normans after 1066 brought little in the way of new population; they came as a conquering aristocracy taking over and altering existing estates. There may have been some settlements in the Fens but elsewhere the Norman elements were small. Nevertheless names such as Norton may reveal some pockets of French settlement, and some of the towns saw Norman influence as at Stamford (Portland) and Lincoln (Newport).

Anglo-Saxon carving, Branston

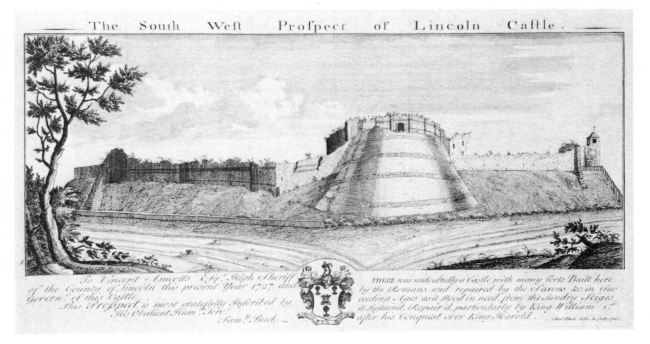

The South West Prospect of Lincoln Castle.

To Vincent Amcotts Esq.: High Sheriff
of the County of Lincoln this present Year 1727, and
Govern.r of this Castle
This Prospect is most gratefully Inscribed by.
His Obedient Hum.ble Ser.t
Sam.ll Buck —

THERE was undoubtedly a Castle with many Forts Built here
by the Romans, and repaired by the Saxons &c. in Suc
ceeding Ages as it stood in need, from the Sundry Sieges
it Sustaind, Repair'd, particularly by King William 1.st
after his Conquest over King Harold.

Sam.l Buck delin & Sculp 1741.

10. A drawing of Lincoln Castle by Buck, 1727.

11. Somerton Castle, near Boothby Graffoe; built 1281.

12. Probably the finest tower and spire in the county: St Wulfram's, Grantham.

13. Some of the fine 14th-century detail of the porch of Heckington Church.

14. The Close Wall, Lincoln: the cathedral and the the buildings which belonged to it were defended against attack during the Middle Ages.

15. Norman house, Steep Hill, Lincoln, one of a series of 12th-century stone houses which reveal the wealth of the town at this period.

16. High Bridge, Lincoln.

V The Middle Ages: Land and Society

Creating the county

The counties of Anglo-Saxon England, each one under an earl, a sheriff and a bishop, were laid out in the ninth and 10th centuries from the south-west, so that the territory attached to the county town usually lay rather to the north and north-east. When those who created them came to the land of the Five Boroughs they found a region already heavily provincialised; each of the towns had a territory which supported it, and as late as the 940s they formed a confederation under an ealdorman and a king's reeve. These arrangements may be reflected in that Nottingham's lands and Derby's lands shared the same sheriff in the Middle Ages.

Perhaps the same originally happened in Lincolnshire. Certainly Lincoln was not only given its own territory of Lindsey to the north and east which already existed under its own ealdorman, but it also received lands to the south including the borough of Stamford. It is not clear if a Stamfordshire ever existed; if so, the process of shiring would suggest that it was Kesteven to the north and east of Stamford. But from as early as we can see, this area came under the authority of the sheriff at Lincoln. Lincolnshire was a double county, with lands both north and south of the city to support it.

One reason for this may have been the loss of part of Stamford's lands by the creation about 963 of the soke of Peterborough out of the lands which belonged to the abbey, and by the formalisation of Rutland, the private possession of the Mercian royal family, as an extra-county territory. This land without any major borough to defend it broke the natural boundary of the county, so that not only did Stamford lie at the very edge of Lincolnshire on a peninsula jutting into the neighbouring counties at a point where four authorities met but parts of the town itself lay in Northamptonshire, in the liberty of the abbot of Peterborough and in Rutland, as well as in Lincolnshire.

But a more likely cause was the sudden savage threat from the new pagan kingdom set up at York in the 930s and 940s by Norse from Dublin. The new English rulers, faced with repelling invaders from the Danelaw (943) and with conquering the north and defending the realm from further incursions, chose Lincoln as their front-line capital, giving that city a double region for support. There is no proof of this, but no other explanation of the double county is satisfactory. It is worthy of note that in due course York too received a multiple territory to support it.

But the different units remained distinct. The Parts of Kesteven,

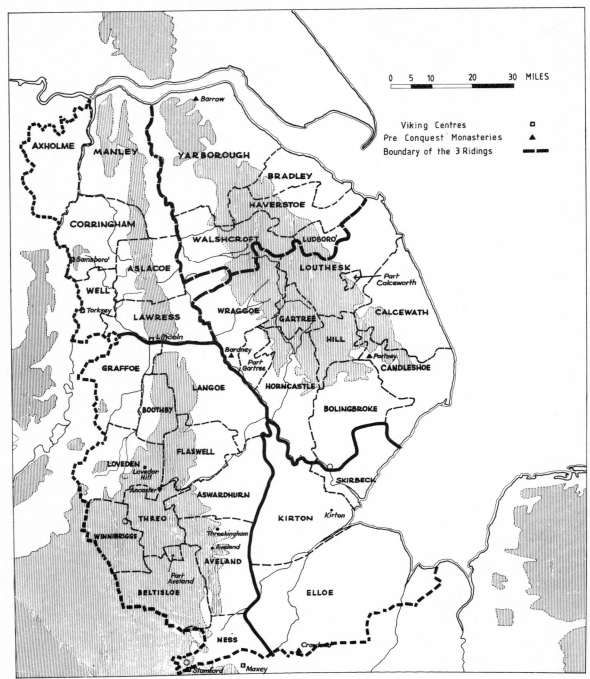

10. Local government in early Lincolnshire.

42

Lindsey and Holland all existed before Domesday Book (1086). Kesteven, heavily wooded (the name includes the British word -*ceto* for forest), reached from Stamford to the Witham at Lincoln, while Lindsey covered all the land to the north and east of Lincoln, probably rather more than the early kingdom. Holland, which seems to have consisted of little more than the area around Kirton, was being reclaimed from the salt and freshwater marshes to the east.

Despite the size of the county, Lincolnshire was a unit. The 'men of Lincolnshire' are referred to in 1086 and on later occasions. There was one shire court which met every six weeks under the sheriff in Lincoln castle. But there was also a court for Kesteven which met at Ancaster and perhaps elsewhere, and the 'men of Kesteven' are mentioned. When justices of the peace were set up, separate benches were commissioned for Lindsey, Kesteven and Holland. And Kesteven and Holland disputed long over their respective boundaries.

Beneath the three parts, Lindsey like Yorkshire had three 'ridings'. Each county had 'wapentakes', groupings of townships; these were the effective units of local government in medieval Lincolnshire. They were well established by the time of Domesday Book, and most of their names like Langoe, Threo and Aveland are Danish though some are English. They varied in size. Kesteven had 11 with an average of 26 townships in each. In Holland they tended to be larger, three covering 51 townships and their extensive fenland territories. Lindsey had 19, varying in size from 18 to 54 townships. On occasion regrouping of villages between wapentakes took place. Each had a court held probably every four weeks; most meeting places were out of doors (Loveden Hill, Aveland in Aslackby parish, Elloe stone in Moulton parish) though some wapentakes had villages with cognate names (Candlesby, Wragby).

Domesday Lincolnshire

Lincolnshire was one of the wealthiest regions in Domesday England. It was already heavily populated. There were more people per acre than in any other county except Norfolk or Suffolk; indeed taking into account the wastelands of fen and heath, the county was probably one of the most densely settled areas of William's new kingdom. And this population lived in nucleated villages, not hamlets or farmsteads. Some 750 villages are mentioned in Domesday Book. Some have now vanished but most of the present villages of the county are recorded; only in the fenlands have significant numbers of new settlements been established since 1086.

The southern Wolds harboured the densest population in large villages, the biggest in the county. The Danish settlement here seems to have been so heavy that secondary infilling was not common. The centre of Kesteven was also heavily settled. In both areas small irregular parishes tell the same story, of villages jostling each other in their demand for land. On the other hand, the clay basins of the Trent, Witham and Ancholme were less densely occupied, and in the Marsh

Barton on Humber church

43

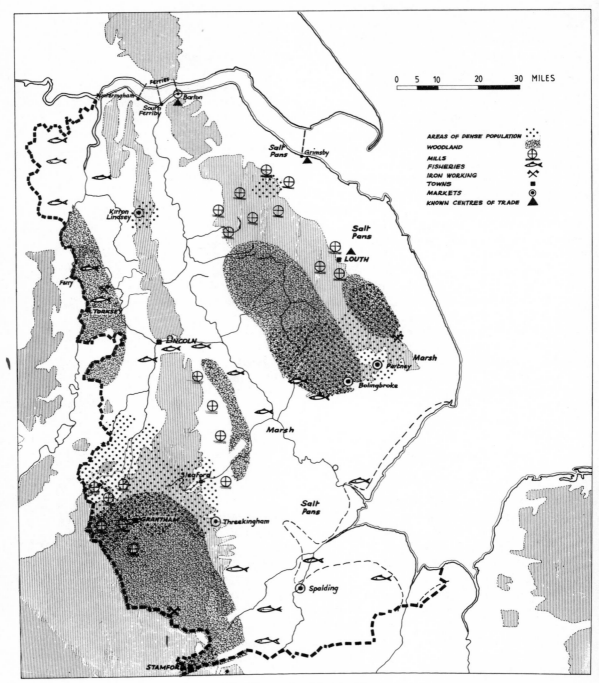

Legend:
AREAS OF DENSE POPULATION
WOODLAND
MILLS
FISHERIES
IRON WORKING
TOWNS
MARKETS
KNOWN CENTRES OF TRADE

0 5 10 20 30 MILES

Ferries
Winteringham
South Ferriby
Barton
Salt Pans
Grimsby
Kirton Lindsey
Salt Pans
LOUTH
Ferry
Torksey
LINCOLN
Partney
Bolingbroke
Marsh
Marsh
Sleaford
Salt Pans
GRANTHAM
Threekingham
Spalding
STAMFORD

11. Domesday Lincolnshire.

44

dispersed settlements appeared early, nucleated villages later. In the Fens, isolated villages, often quite large, lay along the silt bank.

Lincolnshire had not been devastated like Yorkshire by the conquerors; there are few signs of destruction in 1086. The county was however heavily taxed. Kesteven and Holland were probably assessed at first as one unit; they paid rather more than Lindsey, and subsequently some allowances were made to ease Kesteven's burden. It was not until later that the Marsh and Fens became 'the richest part of twelfth-century England'.

The general picture is of a farming community. Most Lincolnshire villages seem to have cultivated two large arable fields, shared among the peasant farmers; as the Middle Ages progressed, the number of fields increased to three or more. Villages had interests in the marshes often many miles away for meadows, pastures, peat pits and saltpans as well as for fish and fowl. River fisheries were highly valued. There was much woodland, especially in the Wolds south of Louth, the vale between Lincoln and the southern Wolds as far as Tattershall, and central Kesteven; these areas are still forested but largely as a result of 18th- and 19th-century plantation. Waste was recorded on the heath and near the coast still liable to flood. Saltpans occur in the Marsh and Fens, and watermills appear, often in large groups (14 at Tealby, 13 at Louth, nine at Nettleton, eight at Sleaford).

The county possessed two major towns, Lincoln and Stamford. Lincoln suffered from the conquest; by 1086 its population had fallen from about 6000 to about 4500; at least 166 houses had been destroyed for a large castle (five acres) in the upper city and work had begun on the new cathedral. Population and the centre of the town had moved downhill to the lower city where an estate of 36 houses and two churches was being developed. Although it had extensive fields, it was an urban community, a focus of trade with Scandinavia and elsewhere, with moneyers and a sophisticated local government based on lawmen. Although the canal between Lincoln and the Trent was blocked until recut in the reign of Henry I, Torksey at the junction of the Fosse Dyke and the Trent was described as a 'suburb of Lincoln'; it had decayed considerably between 1066 and 1086 but was still responsible for conducting king's messengers to York on demand. Stamford too was a major settlement. Soon after the conquest a castle was built, and probably a new market place laid out. It had moneyers and lawmen.

There are signs of other towns, trade and industry in 1086. The king's manor of Grantham had burgesses; with its 'hall' and church, it formerly belonged to Edward the Confessor's queen Edith. Louth had a 'hall' of the bishop of Lincoln, burgesses and a market. Boston does not appear in Domesday – until archaeologists can show that it was omitted we must assume that it grew up after 1086. Markets existed at Bolingbroke and Partney in the southern Wolds, Barton on Humber and perhaps Kirton in the north and at Spalding in the Fens, and a fair at Threekingham in mid-Kesteven. Tolls on shipping were taken at Grimsby, Saltfleet and Barton. Iron-working continued in the Bytham area.

Pottery jug

45

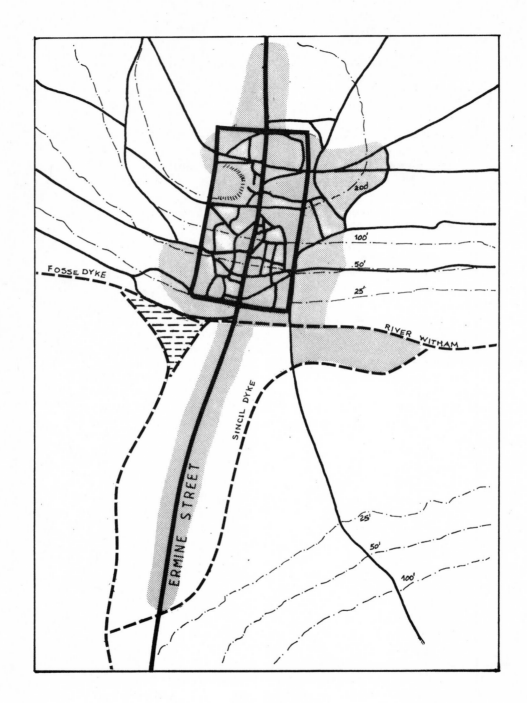

FOSSE DYKE

RIVER WITHAM

ERMINE STREET

SINCIL DYKE

200'

100'

50'

25'

25'

50'

100'

12. Medieval Lincoln.

Social structure

Domesday Book reveals a Norman nobility dominating a mixed Anglo-Norman peasantry. Virtually all pre-conquest landowners in Lincolnshire had been displaced by landlords from Brittany, Flanders or Normandy. Sixty-six tenants-in-chief are listed in Lincolnshire in 1086; only two were English and only one, Colswein of Lincoln, still held his lands and indeed had increased them, perhaps in return for some act of support to the Conqueror. The smaller tenants, both the king's thegns and the sub-tenants of the greater lords, were often Anglo-Danish. There were a few French settlers concentrated in one or two centres. But there was no wholesale dispossession.

Boothby Pagnell manor house

There were 10 ecclesiastical lords like the bishop of Lincoln and they held nearly 20 manors each. The 56 temporal lords averaged twelve and a half manors. Few monasteries held property in Lincolnshire and only one (Peterborough) had extensive lands; Crowland was the only monastery within the borders of the county in 1086. The king had estates throughout the area, in particular the town and soke of Grantham. Already some barons had begun to grant parts of their land to the knights who had fought at Hastings or who came over from the continent later.

One form of estate prominent in Domesday Lincolnshire was the soke, an area of privileged jurisdiction usually administered from a central residence. Some were large, some small; many were centred on English rather than Danish settlements – Edenham, Ruskington, Horncastle. Some like Grantham were made up of scattered estates, others were more compact – some may even have been decaying by 1086.

Beneath the sokes and knights fees were manors, often with outlying *berewicks* (barley-lands or granges). In Lincolnshire the majority of villages were divided between manors; relatively few manors and villages coincided. They were still largely in the hands of Anglo-Danish farmers, but there are signs of new halls and home farms being created to accommodate the Norman newcomers.

Lincolnshire possessed an abnormally large number of free peasants, *sokemen*. They were freer but not necessarily richer than their neighbours. Nearly a half of all sokemen recorded for the country were in Lincolnshire; and more than a half of the county's population fell into this class, some 11,000 in all, and within the larger sokes the proportion was higher (71 per cent in Bolingbroke). The highest concentration lay in the North Riding of Lindsey, with the South Riding next; Kesteven and the West Riding had just under half, while in Holland, the traditional home of the free peasant, there were relatively few. No other county had this concentration, although East Anglia had large proportions of freemen. If sokemen are a sign of Danish settlement, the centre of Scandinavian influence lay in Lincolnshire and it thinned out northwards, westwards and southwards.

Other evidence of Scandinavian influence appears in Domesday –

47

personal names, words like wapentake, carucate and bovate instead of the hundred, ploughland and oxgang, the lawmen of Lincoln and Stamford, the long hundred (120 units) and *ora* (silver ounce worth 16d) and the assessment of geld in blocks of 12 or 24 rather than tens.

Alongside the sokemen, the villeins (landed peasantry) and bordars or cottars (smallholders, landless labourers and craftsmen) were concentrated on manors outside the sokes, and as early as 1086 it was clear that they were more closely tied to their lords than the sokemen.

Castles and lordships

The new lords demanded more dues and services and exploited their new estates more fully. They developed mills, fisheries and salterns. They built substantial stone houses like the later Boothby Pagnell, 'the most important small Norman manor house in England'. Castles accommodating a garrison as well as a lord's household were built by the king at Lincoln and Stamford and by the count of Aumale at Bytham, and more followed in the 12th century. Between 30 and 40 were erected in the county, most during the troubled years of Stephen's reign. Few were in towns – Horncastle, Boston and Grantham seem never to have had castles. Lincoln, Stamford and Sleaford (the bishop of Lincoln's fortress) played important parts in the civil wars between Matilda and Stephen (Stephen was captured at Lincoln in 1141) and in the wars of Henry II and John; John was passing across the Fens (where he lost his baggage and funds on a treacherous causeway) to Swineshead abbey or castle, Sleaford castle and Newark castle where he died. At first strongholds in a conquered countryside, they became fortresses to oppose rivals and to resist the king, residences and administrative centres for far-flung estates; from here the lord's tenants were summoned to his court.

About a third of all William's tenants in chief had estates in Lincolnshire. Some 20 had their *caput* or headquarters in the county. The rest like the earl of Richmond and the bishop of Bayeux ran their Lincolnshire property from centres outside the county. Thus knights from Lincolnshire owed 'castle-ward' at Rockingham (Northants), Richmond (Yorks), Lancaster or elsewhere.

The two most important centres in the region were Lincoln and Bolingbroke. The earls of Chester claimed to be earls of Lincoln and hereditary constables of Lincoln castle; they built a fortress at Bolingbroke, the centre of a lordship with some 60 sub-tenants, one of the county's greatest sokes. Other barons had residences in Lincolnshire. Gilbert de Ghent (whose father had built a castle at Barton in the reign of Stephen) made Folkingham castle his centre, and at Bourne Baldwin fitz Gilbert turned the parish church into a monastery, built a castle and probably laid out a new market place in trying to make a *caput* worthy of the king's relative. Ivo Tailbois the notorious sheriff of Lincolnshire created a home-town at Spalding. The Mowbray family had a castle at Kinnard Ferry and perhaps later at Epworth to control their

17. Tattershall Castle.

18. Harlaxton Manor.

19. Sir Christopher Wray, Lord Chief Justice in 1574 he came from Glentworth, and was an encloser o open lands.

20. Memorial to Peregrine Bertie, 10th Lord Willoughby (died 1601), and his daughter (died 1610) in Spilsby Church.

21. Watermill at Alvingham, one of many processing the agricultural produce of Lincolnshire.

22. Read's Grammar School, Corby, one of a number of schools and almshouses founded in the late 17th century on the growing wealth of the agricultural interest.

23. Gunby Hall, near Skegness (built 1700). One of a number of great houses built on the wealth of 18th-century agriculture.

24. Interior of Wesley's chapel, Raithby, built by Robert Carr Brackenbury in 1799.

25. Fulstow Methodist chapel (formerly Primitive Methodist), built in 1836 and still in use.

26. The Church of England revival: St Helen's church, Saxby, built *c.* 1775.

Axholme estate, and from this refuge they played a part in the struggles of Henry II and Henry III. The Bardolfs built Carlton and the Gresleys Swineshead. Mounds suggestive of motte and bailey castles survive at Corby, Dalby and Barrow. Henry II took measures to deal with unlicensed castle-building, and some like the Amundeville castle at Kingerby were destroyed.

But the royal castles soon passed into private hands, Lincoln to the earls of Lincoln and later the dukes of Lancaster, Stamford to the Humets and then the Warennes. The works never finished at Grimsby may have been intended by the king to restore royal influence, and later Edward I acquired Somerton castle south of Lincoln from the bishop of Durham ('perhaps the finest castle in the county but founded to fulfil no real need of defence or administration') as a royal centre; it served as a prison for the king of France (1359-60) and then fell into decay.

As the Middle Ages advanced, titles and estates became amalgamated until in the 14th century there were about 40 lords in England compared with 180 under William I. The sphere of influence moved from the estate to the shire, and new landholders aspiring to the status of castle dweller emerged – the Moultons of Moulton, the Tatteshales of Tattershall, the Umfravilles of South Kyme. A few of the older centres like Bytham retained their importance, but Lincoln became local government offices, a gaol and a refuge for the Jews in their persecutions. Bolingbroke became a residence until the 1370s when it became the administrative centre for the duchy of Lancaster, and Stamford, Welbourne and Bourne fell into decay.

By the 15th century, Folkingham and Tattershall were the important centres locked in the conflict of their lords Beaumont and Cromwell. Each built up a body of retainers, men who were J.P.s, sheriffs, M.P.s, like Sir Hugh Witham of Boston and Sir William Tailbois of South Kyme who called himself the 'earl of Kyme'; and each looked to greater magnates, the dukes of York or Suffolk, to maintain them in their struggle for influence. There was no permanent grouping of allies; each man sought 'good lordship' where he could find it.

And thus was Lincolnshire involved in the Wars of the Roses. There were uprisings at Grantham and elsewhere in the 1450s. Grantham and Stamford were sacked in 1461 because they belonged to the duke of York. The lords Willoughby and Welles led a disastrous revolt against Edward IV in 1470 at the instigation of the earl of Warwick. There was considerable disorder and violence in the county.

Agriculture

Throughout the Middle Ages Lincolnshire remained one of the most densely occupied regions of England; as the country's population trebled between 1066 and 1300, the county with its waste land was able to absorb more than its share of this increase. Colonisation in the forests of Kesteven and on the lighter soils of the Wolds took place; even the dry lands received their settlements (Temple Bruer on the heath). Whole

Tattershall Castle

Kyme Castle

49

villages as at Brauncewell and Broxholme moved to suit changes in climate, while others shrank or disappeared (Fordington). Reclamation of the wetlands became rapid in the 11th and 12th centuries, reaching its peak in the 13th century. Some was sponsored by religious houses like Crowland, Spalding and the Gilbertines, some by lay magnates; but much was done by the free peasantry either individually or in groups:

> Concerning this marsh a wonder has happened in our time. In years past, these places were accessible neither to man nor beast, affording only deep mud with sedge and reeds, and inhabited by birds . . . This is now changed into delightful meadows and also arable land.

The Isle of Axholme, the Ancholme valley, the Witham basin both east and west of the heathlands and the salt sea marshes all felt the demand for land, but the greatest gains were made in the Marsh, where streams were embanked and sea walls built, and in the Fens where population probably became denser than anywhere else outside the towns. The villages of Moulton and Weston, for instance, which apparently had some 77 households in 1086 had 389 households in 1259-60. Groups of villages often shared the work and the profits, and outlying settlements, some with their own chapels, were established. The meadows and intercommoning of pasture reveal the value of the new lands. Spalding, Crowland and Deeping St James lived in a triangular state of perpetual hostility, quarrelling, raiding and destroying each other's dykes, boundary posts and herds, and there was a similar long-drawn-out struggle between Grimsby and Clee. The Black Death and later plagues were perhaps less sharply felt in Holland than elsewhere in the county where some villages were permanently deserted; it was flooding, beginning in the 1280s, but damaging from the late 14th and 15th centuries which seems to have halted the process of colonisation and even undone the work, despite the efforts of the Commissions of Sewers.

Elsewhere, large estates grew up in Kesteven and on the Wolds, some monastic (Vaudey, Revesby), some lay (Folkingham, Bolingbroke), nucleated villages of owner-occupiers or substantial tenant farmers on the lower clay lands, and areas of dispersed farmsteads in the fenlands, marshes and some forest areas. Some lords kept a tight hold over their tenants as at Scrivelsby (Marmions, later Dymokes), Stow by Lincoln (the bishop), Baston and Langtoft (Crowland). Fairs were established as at Stow Green by Sempringham abbey. Other villages were less strongly manorialised like Heckington. On big estates like the bishopric of Lincoln or the duchy of Lancaster, a new breed of estate administrators emerged, increasing the range of management experience within the local community.

The land was fully exploited. There was salt-making, fowling and fishing in the wetlands and rabbit warrens, pottery and quarrying elsewhere, leather processing in the south west. Corn was grown everywhere, even on the new lands, so that in some places pasture became scarce. But by the 13th century the main produce was wool. The long-woolled sheep bred from Yorkshire to Northamptonshire produced the best wool in Europe. In the Fens, flocks running into thousands of sheep were kept by lay magnates and the larger monasteries, and every religious house and almost every peasant had some income from wool. In 1300 an Italian directed fellow merchants to the Lindsey Wolds for the best wool. The yields and quality of the produce of the sheep walks were equalled only in the Cotswolds and on the Welsh Marches. Sometimes whole village communities were removed to make way for sheep, and the wool-house, mill and tannery at Vaudey abbey reveal something of the wealth and economic activities of a typical Lincolnshire monastery.

Most of this wool was exported, principally through the ports of the Wash. Lincolnshire towns like Lincolnshire peasants thrived on the backs of their sheep. A larger proportion of the county's population lived in towns than in other areas. Lincoln was for much of the time the second city of the realm, and Boston was a boom town, the greatest port after London despite fire, floods and riots; indeed Boston and Lincoln together probably had more trade than London. Stamford was a great trading centre, Grantham, Grimsby and Louth sizeable market towns, Saltfleetby and Wainfleet active havens. Throughout the county smaller market towns flourished. New towns grew up, some like Crowland round monasteries, others like Bourne round a castle. Barton developed at the ferry and remained important until it lost the river trade to Hull. One or two towns were planned – New Sleaford by the bishop of Lincoln and perhaps Tattershall and Gainsborough, but the movement to found new towns was weaker in Lincolnshire than elsewhere.

Wainfleet market cross

The towns had little political influence. Very few apart from Lincoln and Grimsby had M.P.s until the 15th century, not even Boston. Their power was trade. Lincoln grew to some 7000 population. The walls were repaired and extended; with the town's fields to the north, church lands (Monks Liberty) to the east and private land to the south (Malandry), suburbs sprang up at Newport to the north, Wigford to the south, Newland in the west and Thorngate (the home of foreign merchants) to the south east. Downhill lay most of the churches and markets, while the upper city housed the castle and the ever-growing cathedral. With its famous Lincoln scarlets, grains (red, not green), says and blanchets, it was an industrial centre, the third city of the realm, exceeded by London and equalled by York. Parliament met here on several occasions.

Three of England's five international marts were at Boston, Stamford and St Ives nearby, while a fourth lay at Northampton in the county's hinterland. King's Lynn, like Lincoln, was a focus for international trade. Merchants came with furs, fish, hawks, timber and metal goods; cloth, linen, dyes and canvas came from Flanders, spices and wine from Gascony and the south. Italian and Spaniard found goods they needed at these fairs; they took away English corn and malt, lead from Derbyshire and salt, above all wool and cloth. One third of England's wool exports passed through Boston, from the Midlands and as far as the Welsh border, the clippings of some three million sheep. Most went to

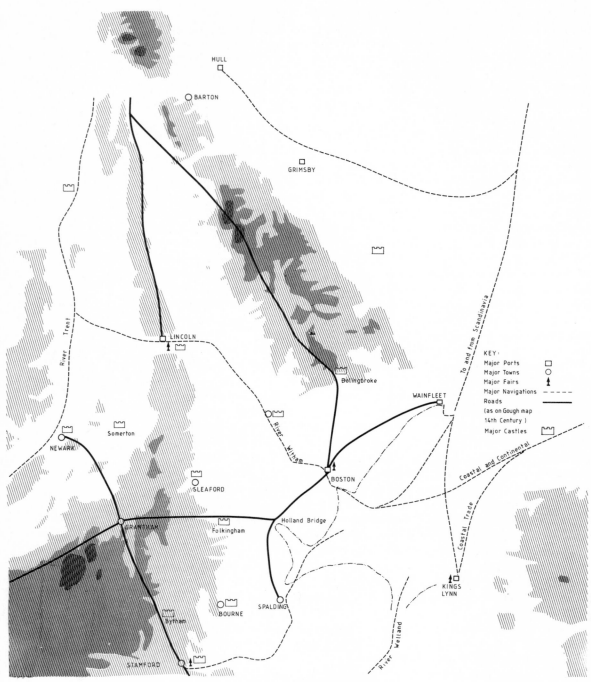

KEY:
Major Ports ☐
Major Towns ○
Major Fairs ⬆
Major Navigations ----
Roads
(as on Gough map
14th Century)
Major Castles ⬚

HULL

BARTON

GRIMSBY

River Trent

LINCOLN

Bolingbroke

WAINFLEET

To and from Scandinavia

Coastal and Continental

Coastal Trade

Somerton

NEWARK

SLEAFORD

River Witham

BOSTON

GRANTHAM

Folkingham

Holland Bridge

KINGS LYNN

BOURNE

SPALDING

Bytham

STAMFORD

River Welland

13. Medieval Lincolnshire.

Flanders but nearly a sixth reached Italy. The trade was largely in the hands of foreigners; most of the ships belonged to alien merchants, but native merchants exported wool from Hull and Lynn as well as Boston – in 1296-7 there were 34 alien shippers in Boston and five native shippers.

Much of the wool was purchased directly from the producers. It was the cloth merchants who frequented the fairs for fine Flemish cloth, brightly coloured and carefully finished, the best in Europe. Most of the cloth for the royal household was bought at the Lincolnshire fairs rather than at Winchester. But the buyers came for the products of Stamford and Lincoln as well as of Ypres and Ghent, for the fairs were at the centre of England's own cloth industry in a region which stretched from York to Leicester; the Lincoln and Stamford cloths may have been made in those towns or in the villages around and sold in the towns but they dominated the market.

By the 14th century, decline set in. As early as 1179 Lincoln had received a first blow to its prosperity when Newark bridge was built over the Trent despite a condition that 'it may not harm my city of Lincoln'; the main route to the north was diverted from Lincoln to pass through Grantham and Newark, and Lincolnshire's county town became isolated. The first road map (Gough's map) shows Lincoln with a road north to the Humber but no road south. The expulsion of the Jews with their systems of credit and trade a century later resulted in considerable economic distress in the city.

But more than all was the fall off in the wool trade. The king regulated the trade and for a time Lincoln and then Boston became 'staple' ports, charged with collecting the heavy duties on the export of wool, but in the end this moved to Calais. Plague, depopulation and the French wars all contributed to the decline. The general pattern of trade in Europe changed and Lincolnshire, closely tied to the northern markets since the 10th century, suffered as the merchants of Norway and Gascony gave way to the more restrictive merchants of the Hanse and Italy. The Germans left their mark on Boston church, and most of the wool went south rather than east as the markets of the north became closed, although Boston merchants tried to keep open the routes to Iceland in the 15th century. The salt industry declined until in 1364 coal and cloth were exchanged for salt from southern France; the surviving salterns supplied local markets only. With the salt the fishing industry declined, and piracy and wrecking became a major occupation for the coast dwellers, especially the men of Grimsby.

And the cloth industry moved. By the late 14th century worsteds and other cloths were being made in west Yorkshire, East Anglia and the west Midlands. Some of the new cloths from Coventry were exported through Boston (although it was silting up) and local wool merchants were still wealthy like the Browne family of Stamford who founded Browne's hospital. Many agricultural areas remained prosperous but the towns declined. Lincoln suffered most; it became a remote country town, cut off from the main water and land routes (the Fosse Dyke was often blocked and the Witham silted up). Stamford, Barton and Grantham retained some of their prosperity into the 16th century, and links with the continent persisted – the 'Dutch' for instance were busy building at Thornton, Tattershall and Boston; but the great days of Lincolnshire as a major focus of Europe's trade were over.

Thornton Curtis Abbey gatehouse

VI The Middle Ages: Church and People

Christianity came early to the area and Lincoln was its natural focus. There are a few signs of Christian adherence during the Roman period. Early in the seventh century, as Bede records, Paulinus bishop of York led a mission to

> the province of Lindsey, which is the first on the south side of the river Humber, stretching out as far as the sea; and he first converted the governor of the city of Lincoln, whose name was Blecca, with his whole family. He likewise built in that city a stone church of beautiful workmanship.

Converts were baptised in the presence of King Edwin of York in the Trent near Littleborough.

Although Lindsey was conquered by pagan Mercia a few years later, the work of conversion continued. The names of some early missionaries are known, like Chad who founded Barrow, Oswald of Bardney and Higbald abbot of a Lindsey monastery commemorated in the dedication of churches around Hibaldstow (Higbald's shrine). Minster churches — mission stations staffed by a number of clergy who preached in the area around — characterised this early church. A few are known like Threekingham, and vestiges of others can be seen at Grantham, Caistor, Horncastle and at Louth and Stow by Lincoln; St Paulinus' church at Lincoln may also have been one. A few private churches may have been founded as well.

Reader's pulpit, Tupholme Priory

The first diocese

By about 680 the kingdom of Lindsey had its own bishop owing allegiance to York or Lichfield depending on whether Northumbria or Mercia wielded authority over the area. His seat was at 'Sidnacester', the site of which is unknown. South Lincolnshire lay in the diocese or sub-diocese of Leicester with general allegiance to Lichfield.

This structure was destroyed when the Danes came. There ceased to be a bishop in Lindsey; the bishop of Leicester had responsibility for the whole area. As pressure from the Danes increased he gradually withdrew to Dorchester on Thames. But Christianity survived the new pagan settlement, and when the Danelaw was conquered by Wessex, the conversion of its inhabitants was rapid. The region produced a number of bishops, and the relative absence of pagan burials and the presence of Christian symbols on coins suggest a swift and deep response. When the area was once again rescued from York rule in the mid-10th century, it was regarded as the rescue of a Christian population from a pagan overlord.

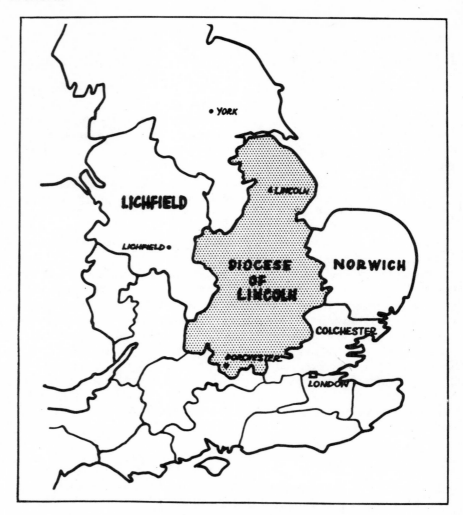

14. The medieval diocese.

The medieval diocese

The whole area from the Thames to the Humber thus came under the bishop of Dorchester with perhaps suffragan bishops; in 991 there is mention of 'the men of Kesteven and their bishop Aeswige'. Soon after the Conquest, along with other bishops, Remigius the new Norman bishop at Dorchester moved his see; he chose Lincoln, perhaps in response to claims by the archbishop of York to jurisdiction over Lindsey and ownership of estates at Louth, Stow, Newark and elsewhere. Al-

56

though the Council of Winchester in 1072 had ruled in favour of Remigius, York objected to his move to Lincoln, claiming that the bishop was now resident in the northern province. The dispute was a long one with the king and pope supporting Remigius, but the cathedral was dedicated in 1095 despite protests from the archbishop and the diocese of Lincoln remained in this form until the Reformation.

The religious life of the diocese and especially of the county focussed on Lincoln. Remigius started the cathedral and his work can still be seen in the west front. But this work was destroyed by fire in 1141 and its successor by earthquake in 1185. The present church and chapter house are largely the result of work started in 1192 by Hugh, Bishop of Lincoln, and lasting until 1232. The cathedral was extended across the Roman city wall to the east and the central tower was capped by a spire (removed in the 16th century). The Angel Choir was built 1260-80. The result is probably the finest early Gothic building in Europe, a symbol of religious domination and achievement. Round it lies the Close with its houses for canons, Vicars Court and the bishop's palace.

Louth church

Apart from Lincoln, the bishop had a palace at Stow, a house at Nettleham and a castle at Sleaford in Lincolnshire; but his main residences lay outside of the region at Newark castle, Buckden palace and elsewhere. Many bishops of Lincoln, like Richard Gravesend (1258-79), served the king in various capacities throughout the Middle Ages. But despite his absences, the bishop directed the religious life of the diocese, often at the instance of the king or pope. He supervised the clergy and sought to control the lay patrons who appointed them; he regulated the monasteries and issued orders concerning church buildings and lay morals; he set up councils and synods and visited the diocese area by area; he built up a body of officials and an administrative system. The huge diocese was divided into seven archdeaconries roughly coinciding with the nine counties covered. Lincolnshire was sub-divided, the archdeaconry of Stow covering the area of Lindsey and based on Remigius' new monastery at Stow, and the archdeaconry of Lincoln covering the rest of the county. Courts were held and officials such as sequestrators for the probate of wills appointed. By about 1100, Lincolnshire was further divided into 25 deaneries, approximating to the wapentakes, each with its dean and chapter of clergy.

Churches

Few if any pre-Danish churches survived the invasions, and our present parish churches were founded after the conversion of the Danelaw. By 1086 a third of all the parish churches in the county had been established and the number may have been higher, for pre-Conquest work survives in some churches not mentioned in Domesday Book. Some places like Binbrook and Threekingham had two churches, perhaps representing twin settlements (North and South Elkington, East and West Allington). The number recorded for Lincolnshire, 255 in 248 places, is higher than for any other county save Suffolk; Norfolk with 243 churches comes next.

57

Since parish churches were built and endowed by owners of private estates, there was over-provision in some areas, especially in the towns. Medieval Lincoln had 48 churches, Stamford fourteen. But Boston, Louth, Grantham and Grimsby had only one or two medieval churches, reflecting the pattern of ownership in these places. In the countryside, churches continued to be established until about 1150, some remaining as private chapels or chapels of ease, others becoming parish churches.

Parishes were created by attaching to a church an area, usually based on an estate or township, which paid its tithes to that church and enjoyed its spiritual services. They varied in size, some covering more than one village, others only part of a village territory. New parishes were formed by sub-dividing earlier parishes. In the southern Wolds and central Kesteven where villages were close together and landlordship strong, parishes were small and irregular in shape; along the edges of the limestone belt, the parishes included different types of land, high heath-land, low clay pastures and meadows. In the Fens and Marsh, the undrained land was divided, sometimes at a late date by drawing straight lines across empty areas where inhabitants of neighbouring settlements grazed their cattle in common.

There are few second-rate medieval churches in Lincolnshire; even the smallest village lavished care on its religious centre. With good building materials, long architectural traditions and skilled craftsmen to hand, Lincolnshire produced the richest architectural harvest in the country. Local schools of building styles can be seen, as in the Sleaford area, while the Lincolnshire broach spire is rivalled only by that of the Nene valley.

The surviving buildings reflect the wealth and devotion of those who gave to the fabric, furniture and ritual of the churches which dominated the landscape. During the 14th and 15th centuries, guilds and private chantries were founded in town and village churches alike; altars were set up and priests endowed to pray for the soul of members of the guild or the donor's family. Churches were enlarged, often to house several such chantries, and sometimes as at Sedgebrook regulations were drawn up for the chantry priests. Grantham had at least six such altars and more than ten clergy, while Boston, Sleaford, Louth and Gainsborough were served by several priests; even smaller rural churches had more than the statutory priest and deacon. At Spilsby and Tattershall, 'colleges' were founded with clergy living under common rules.

Chapels and hospitals were founded, mostly in the towns. Lincoln had five hospitals, Stamford three, and there were a further 14 in the county, small houses run by monks, canons or nuns to help the poor, the sick, the aged and/or travellers. A few were in villages or like Spittal le Street in the countryside on the main roads.

Monasteries

There were more monasteries in Lincolnshire for its size than in any other county save Yorkshire. They lay scattered over the county, large

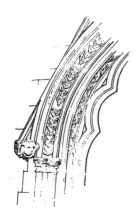

Carving, Ewerby church

Browne's Hospital, Stamford

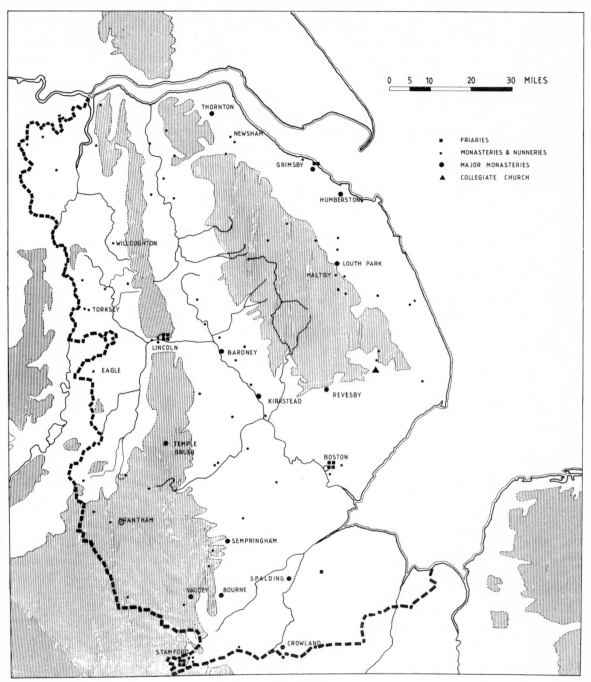

Scale: 0 5 10 20 30 MILES

■ FRIARIES
· MONASTERIES & NUNNERIES
● MAJOR MONASTERIES
▲ COLLEGIATE CHURCH

THORNTON

NEWSHAM

GRIMSBY

HUMBERSTON

WILLOUGHTON

LOUTH PARK

MALTBY

TORKSEY

LINCOLN

BARDNEY

EAGLE

KIRKSTEAD

REVESBY

TEMPLE BRUER

BOSTON

GRANTHAM

SEMPRINGHAM

SPALDING

VAUDEY   BOURNE

STAMFORD

CROWLAND

15. Monastic Houses.

59

ones like Crowland and small ones like Newbo in Sedgebrook. Most have vanished, their stones used for building and for burning for lime to sweeten the soil, especially in the Fens; a number of villages are built from the carved and dressed stone taken from monastic sites (in 18th-century Crowland, 'you see pieces of it in every house', as Stukeley noted). Few sites have been excavated, and thus the remains are not as striking as those of Yorkshire and elsewhere.

One reason for the number of monasteries was the wealth of Lincolnshire. Further, it abounded in freemen who could give land for religious purposes, and there was wasteland for monks seeking solitude. Most of them were founded after the Conquest. All the pre-Danish monasteries, whether refuges or spearheads of evangelisation, were destroyed, and only Crowland was re-occupied when monasteries came to be refounded in the 10th and early 11th centuries. Later legends claim for Spalding and St Leonard's Stamford very early foundations, and the pre-Danish site of Bardney was re-settled in 1087.

From 1066 to 1135, eight monasteries were established in the county, but during Stephen's troubled 19 years no less than 23 houses were set up. Thereafter the rate fell again; 12 were built in 35 years under Henry II and six more from 1180 to 1396. All the orders save the Cluniacs were represented in the area, but the most popular was the Gilbertines. The only English medieval monastic order, it began in Lincolnshire; Gilbert the rector of Sempringham was encouraged by his patron (Gilbert de Ghent of Folkingham) to establish a house for nuns with canons attached. The movement became the most popular order for women in the 12th century; while St Gilbert lived (he died in 1189, aged 105), most houses were double houses but after his death the new foundations tended to be for men only. Most of the 11 Gilbertine monasteries in Lincolnshire were built before 1189, and all but two housed both nuns and canons. A Carthusian house was founded late in the 14th century by the Mowbrays in Axholme. There were five houses of the Knights Templar, joined after their suppression in 1311 to the two smaller Hospitallers centres; Eagle, Aslackby and Witham were important houses, Temple Bruer on the Heath a later foundation.

Most of the monasteries were built by the lesser nobility; five were royal foundations, 13 were established by great magnates and four by bishops, one by 'the men of Torksey'. Some, especially the Cistercians, were no doubt founded on the initiative of groups of monks seeking isolation; Kirkstead was located in a place of 'horror like a vast solitude'. At Revesby and elsewhere whole villages were cleared away, and the monks of Castle Bytham moved to a more private site at Vaudey.

Others were founded by lay lords improving the status of a church or estate. At Bourne, Baldwin fitz Gilbert asked Arrouaise in France to supply canons to man the church he was rebuilding, and elsewhere lords built monasteries close to their main residence – Tailbois at Spalding, Alan de Creoun at Frieston, the count of Aumale at Castle Bytham. Kirkstead looked to the lord of Tattershall nearby for patronage and protection, Revesby to the earl of Lincoln at Bolingbroke. The bishop of Lincoln gave Haverholme close to his castle and new town of Sleaford to the Cistercians, and when they moved to Louth Park in search of better lands he gave it to the Gilbertines, who complained of the isolation and uselessness of the site.

The lesser gentry had similar motives – to improve their lands, establish a memorial for themselves and save their souls by the prayers of a religious community. This accounts for the smaller houses with only three or four monks, daughter houses of larger monasteries. Baldwin fitz Gilbert established Deeping St James and gave it to Thorney abbey. Perpetual intercession could also be secured by granting land to a monastery elsewhere; the 13 or so 'alien priories' in Lincolnshire, cells of continental (mostly French) houses, were founded in this way. Hugh Wake gave land at Wilsford to Bec abbey in Normandy, Ralph of Fougeres granted Long Bennington church to Savigny: in both cases, a small priory was established with a monk-warden and perhaps one other brother but no full monastic residence. Lincolnshire lands were valuable and many monasteries were keen to own such estates; perhaps this accounts for the presence of the early houses on wastelands, the later ones on richer soils.

Lincolnshire had a number of friaries, those shock-troops of the 13th-century church, travelling out from their town head-quarters to preach, beg, resist heresy and serve the disadvantaged. Boston, Lincoln and Stamford had houses of all four main orders, Franciscans (Grey), Dominicans (Black), Carmelites (White) and Austin friars; Grimsby had two, Grantham one, and there was a short-lived house at Whaplode in the Fens.

Folkingham church

Popular religion

Behind the parish church with its rites of baptism, marriage, burial, mass and occasional sermon (most preaching was left to the friars) was a deeply rooted set of religious practices based on local shrines, crosses and holy sites, trees and wells. Sometimes non-parochial chapels came to mark these sites as the frontiers of settlement in the Fens and the forests of Kesteven were pushed back.

Lincoln was at the heart of the religious life of the area. The cult of St Hugh made it for a time as important a devotional centre as Walsingham in Norfolk. No other place in the county rivalled this: Boston with its Holy Rood and monasteries like Crowland and Sempringham set out to attract devotees and their offerings to the building funds. Only Stamford became a major religious centre with its churches, monasteries, hospitals and schools. For a short time in the 1330s there was an attempt to establish a university at Stamford. Students and teachers from Oxford settled there until the king and the bishop of Lincoln at the request of the university at Oxford suppressed this academy, and from this time the schools at Stamford declined.

As the Middle Ages passed, efforts were made to channel popular

61

religion into specifically Christian forms. The bishop of Lincoln paid particular attention to the monasteries where lay patronage and a decline in fervour had led to corruption in some places; at Bardney for instance, the visitors found hounds in the cloisters and mews for hawks. These reforms seem to have had some success, and many Lincolnshire monasteries, especially the smaller ones, were better places in 1530 than they had been a hundred years before.

Crowland
Abbey ruins

VII The Age of Reformation

On Sunday 1 October 1536 armed men under a shoemaker rejoicing in the title Captain Cobbler took possession of Louth parish church. What began as a demonstration developed into a riot, and several of the gentry and clergy became involved. Houses were wrecked, government servants attacked and soon half Lincolnshire was ablaze. Groups of men assembled at Caistor, Louth and Horncastle and 'burned Gaynesborough my lord Burrowe's [Burgh] house and Kyme also'. How much of the county was affected is not clear; Robert Carr in his statement against lord Hussey of Sleaford asserted that 'if my lord had gathered men for the King as he has done for his own pomp to ride to sessions or assize, he might have driven back the rebels', but Hussey reported to Thomas Cromwell, the king's minister, that even if he had reached the rebels he would not have found anyone in the county to fight for him. Instead troops were mustered outside the area at Nottingham and Huntingdon. The mob was free to march on Sleaford and on Lincoln where they awaited the king's reply to their demands.

The reasons for this rising were mixed. Violence was still prevalent in the countryside; if Robert de la Launde of Ashby could attack the Knights Hospitallers at Temple Bruer, lesser men could oppose a new tax with force. It was not however just the tax which caused the riot; it was the new and more efficient system of government which lay behind the tax, an administration which had ordered parish registers to be kept and with its Statute of Uses had deprived the landholder of his right to leave his lands to anyone he chose. And it could enforce its rule in the counties: commissioners from London enquired into enclosures or local disturbances or evasions of some new law; three sets of commissioners were assembled near Louth when the rising broke out, commissioners for the suppression of the monasteries, tax commissioners at Caistor and commissioners to visit the clergy of Louth and Horncastle. Such rulers brought swift and harsh suppression; by 13 October the rising had collapsed, though Robert Aske, one of its leaders, fled into Yorkshire to lead the Pilgrimage of Grace later. Twenty-one ringleaders, commons and clergy, were executed including the abbots of Kirkstead and Barlings; even Hussey was beheaded for doing nothing. When the king passed through the region, he was met by sullen 'quietness'.

Poverty

What he saw was not the rich region of earlier days. Grantham and Stamford still flourished, Boston maintained its position for a time and some of the larger fenland communities were prosperous. But flooding was destroying whole settlements (Skegness was 'clene consumid and eten up with the se' in 1526) and most of the salterns (in the great flood of 1571 'all the salt-cotes where the chief and finest salt was made were utterly destroyed'), the industrial basis of the county's economy, especially cloth-making, was collapsing, and trade was declining.

The land was still intensively exploited. Lincolnshire's contribution to the nation was the produce of the countryside, from building stone to eels. Arable was now more important than grazing, but pressure was growing for more pasture, for sheep on the Wolds and Heath, for cattle fattening in the clay vales and Marsh, and for dairy and meat in the keenly regulated fen pasturages. There was some depopulation caused by enclosure – 12 villages disappeared in Kesteven, 17 in Lindsey, mostly on the Wolds – but not as much as elsewhere. As the numbers of livestock increased, so too did the cultivation of winter feed crops such as pulses. Everywhere corn and pasture lived side by side. Even in the Fens, despite the flooding, barley was the main crop.

The Pelham family monument

There are signs that the economy of Lincolnshire was slowing down. There are few great Tudor houses in the county – Irnham in the early years and Doddington at the end of the century are exceptions. The others like Stragglethorpe, Halstead, Torksey or Brocklesby are minor examples. There were others now gone – Snarford, Glentworth, Ashby de la Launde, Aubourn, Belleau and the large mansion begun by Lord Clinton on the site of Sempringham abbey, but the county has little to offer in the way of parks and country mansions. When Henry VIII called the rebels 'rude commons of one shire, and that one of the most brute and beastly of the whole realm', he was echoing common opinion; his librarian John Leland said that the county, though plentifully supplied with ruins, lacked fine buildings and that the towns were 'much decay'd'.

The towns were certainly suffering. Lincoln's trade had been falling off since two-thirds of its population had died in the Black Death and subsequent plagues in the 14th century; by the mid-16th century the town probably housed only some 2,500. Buildings were empty, streets blocked by fallen house timbers and the suburbs had dwindled; by 1549 only half the number of parish churches were left. Those who later visited the city spoke of its sorry plight – Evelyn (1654) called it 'an old confused town', John Rey (1662) 'a mean and poor place of little trade . . . of no strength and . . . full of tumult'.

Boston was hit by the silting up of its harbour. Stamford did not recover from the dissolution of its religious houses and the decline of its fair for some 200 years, although a number of buildings suggest there was still some wealth in the town; several of its churches were closed by Act of Parliament at this time. By the middle of the century, Lincolnshire no longer possessed any town of national importance. On the other hand, the smaller market towns like Market Deeping, Burgh le Marsh, Tattershall and Ancaster grew. By the 17th century, 34 market centres are recorded in the county, mostly very small (only six had

27. Stamford: the Friday market in Broad Street.

28. Seventeenth and eighteenth-century town houses, Caistor.

29. Illustration of Robey (Lincoln) ploughing tackle, from an export leaflet.

30. A demonstration of steam ploughing in a competition at Louth.

31. A Victorian beam drainage engine at Dogdyke pumping station, Tattershall, dating from 1856.

32. The Ancholme Navigation at Bishopsbridge.

33. Boston Haven and Boston Stump.

34. Grimsby Docks, showing fishing boats and the Dock Tower.

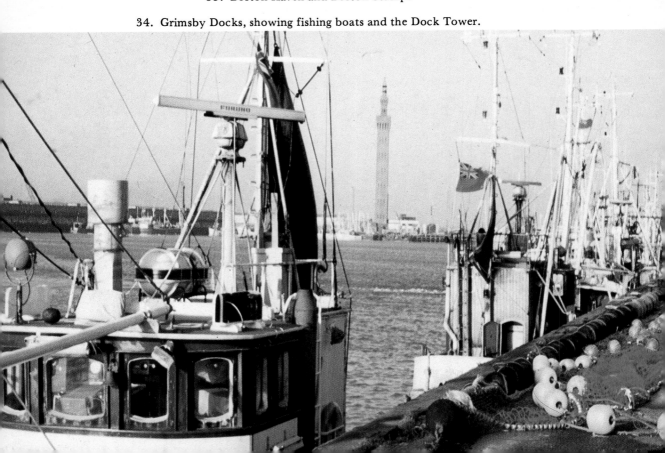

populations larger than 2500); and it was on this network of local trading centres, rather than on a few great towns as existed earlier, that the modern urban pattern has been built.

Religious changes

Lincolnshire's reputation for decay was probably based on the ruins of its monasteries, swept away in the changes made by Henry VIII. In 1534, the smaller houses, of which Lincolnshire had many (a tenth of all monasteries valued at less than £200 p.a. were in the county) were dissolved. In 1536, 36 more monasteries were inspected, found wanting and closed; Cromwell's servants engaged in destroying Legbourne nunnery near Louth only just escaped with their lives. The work of destruction was thorough; the Lincolnshire commissioners were ordered to raze the houses to the ground, and when they complained that 'there be more of great houses in England besides with thick walls and most part of them vaulted', instructions were given to save costs by removing the roofs, gables and stairs, leaving the walls standing; the lead was carried to Lincoln, and the buildings – as at Louth – were given as quarries to local communities.

The closure of the monasteries was only one part of Henry VIII's changes. The old order was to be destroyed. The rebels in Lincolnshire in 1536 intended to stop the process before their parish churches were attacked. But they failed and their fears proved correct. More monasteries were dissolved as a result of the rising and by 1538 they were all gone. When Edward VI came to the throne, the inhabitants of town and country saw their chantries, guilds and plays swept away. Some chapels were closed, a loss felt keenly in some of the huge fenland parishes. Most of the hospitals were dissolved, and there was a struggle to keep the schools, despite the growing demand for them from gentry and merchants. The parish churches felt the winds of change: gold and silver and jewelled ornaments were sold, bells melted, images pulled down, wall paintings whitewashed and replaced by texts, and a number of churches especially in the towns were closed. In some places there was resistance; in others the churchwardens disposed of the church property before it was seized.

Torksey manor house

Nor did the cathedral escape. The shrines of St Hugh and other saints were sacked. In 1547 the recently installed bishop Henry Holbeche surrendered many of the episcopal estates, and large parts of the diocese were given to the new bishoprics of Oxford and Peterborough. It is not surprising that the rebels in 1536 plundered the palace of Bishop John Longland who as confessor to the king was thought to be behind many of these changes.

Social fabric

Some people profited from the changes. John Holland and Richard Glanforthe bought the rich cloth fittings of Winterton church. Monastic lands and buildings were given or sold, sometimes complete. Lord Cecil in the reign of Elizabeth was informed:

> Grimsby Grey Friars – stands whole, nothing sold, Mr. Hatclyff has possession. Grantham Friars is whole by your commandment; [Stamford] Black friars – I think the king would he, should have a dwelling house and the rest be sold for greatest profit. Austin Friars is sold by one Gedney. The White and Gray Friars sold by order of Master Sesel.

About one sixth of the cultivated land of Lincolnshire passed from ecclesiastical into lay ownership at this time.

Ayscough monument

Social changes

The political life of the county was transformed. Until the 1530s there was no dominant figure to consolidate royal power in the region. Lord Beaumont had been mad for many years before he died in 1507, while the lords Willoughby of Parham, Burgh of Gainsborough and Hussey of Sleaford were lesser men; and the crown neglected the Lancaster estate of Bolingbroke. The vacuum allowed the rise of gentry families, some like John Heneage, the bishop's steward, on the basis of office, others on land ownership. The wealthiest were the Ayscoughs of Stallingborough and South Kelsey, the Dymokes of Scrivelsby and the Tyrwhits of Kettleby, but there were many others who could occupy with dignity the role of J.P.s, fewer in the Fens ('the want of gentlemen here to inhabit', 1580) than in Kesteven and particularly on the Wolds.

The rebellion seems to have alerted the king to his weakness in the region. He built up the wealth and power of Charles Brandon duke of Suffolk, his brother in law and favourite who had married Katherine heiress to the Willoughby fortune; Brandon settled at Grimsthorpe and was granted large monastic estates including Vaudey and Louth Park. He dominated the county until his death in 1545. Edward Fiennes lord Clinton and Saye of Tattershall succeeded him from the 1550s; rewarded with large estates, many of them monastic, he became lord lieutenant and from 1572 earl of Lincoln. Both Brandon and Clinton were supported by Thomas Manners first earl of Rutland at Belvoir (another monastic property) on the county border.

Monastic estates were thus used to build up royal influence in the region. Whether this meant change in land use is not clear. Some new owners like the Copledykes of Harrington or Thomas Taylor of Doddington, the bishop's registrar, built houses, and a few like Brandon at Grimsthorpe laid out 'a fayre parke'. Robert Carr, son of a rich merchant and king's steward at Sleaford, 'a proper gentleman', was accused in the Star Chamber of having 'dispossessed the poor inhabitants of their houses, decayed their town and turned the same wholly to sheep . . . pulled down and defaced [three churches] tearing down and spoiling all manner the furnitures and ornaments there'; but it is not clear how typical Carr was.

Not all the older families opposed the new order any more than all the new ones supported it. A pro-Catholic family for instance acquired

Nocton Priory and built a hall there. But the sales, like the marriage of the clergy, created a vested interest in maintaining the Protestant Reformation; there were many opposed to the restoration of the old religion. The puritans Hugh Latimer and John Foxe found their warmest welcome from the duchess of Suffolk at Grimsthorpe, especially after her marriage to Richard Bertie, her gentleman usher.

Such doctrinal convictions were probably rare. Some 81 clergy were ejected from their livings, mostly because they were married. But Mary's reign produced no martyrs in this county. The area was fortunate; Bishop John White who left for Winchester in 1556 burned many heretics while his successor at Lincoln Thomas Watson burned none. Probably most people in the county did like Thomas Armstrong of Corby and his wife, who when convicted of heresy did penance in Lincoln and Grantham churches, but Anthony Meres who was accused of not receiving communion at Easter was one of the many who, led by the duchess of Suffolk, fled into exile.

The exiles returned in 1558 when Elizabeth succeeded her sister. There was little persecution, although the bishop and 11 senior clergy (mostly archdeacons and prebendaries) were in their turn ejected. The county provided only one Catholic martyr, Hugh More, hung in London in 1588, just as it had provided only one Protestant martyr, Ann Askew of Stallingborough, burned in 1546. But the old religion was still strong in the region: 'the common people wolde pontt them [married clergy] with fingers when they saw them'. Lord Burghley was concerned about the entry of 'the obstinate recusants into Lincolnshire [so much so that] part of Lincolnshire is more dangerous than the worst part of Yorkshire'. Gathered in small pockets, these Catholics were supported by gentry families like the Yarboroughs, Tyrwhits, Heneages and Dymokes of the Wolds and the Thimelbys of central Kesteven, who in 1580 baptised their son 'in Poperie [and] uttered badd and unreverend wordes of her Majestie'. Similarly pockets of puritans grew up, for example at Grimsthorpe, and puritan 'preachers' were appointed to some Lincolnshire churches; 23 non-subscribers were suspended in 1583 when archbishop John Whitgift (who came from Grimsby) ordered all clergy and preachers to subscribe to the Book of Common Prayer and the 1562 Articles of Religion.

Most people, however, continued to attend church whatever form of religion prevailed. Like William Cecil, Lord Burghley of Stamford, they were occupied with violence in the towns and countryside or with the state of the local economy. Cecil and the Trollope family were involved in a scheme 'for setting up a mill to knoke hempe for the making of canvas and other linen clothes', and some foreigners were brought in to practise and teach their skills. Plague struck the county in the 1580s and 1590s, checking the growth in population which had begun about the middle of the century. It was death and disease, poverty and abuse, which concerned the bulk of the Lincolnshire peasantry rather than abstruse points of theology.

The Heneage Arms

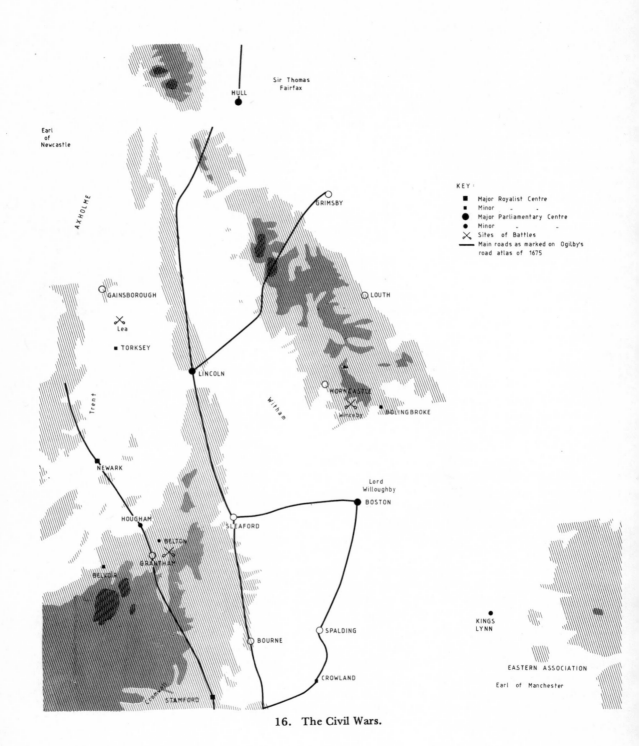

16. The Civil Wars.

VIII The Age of Revolution

The part played by Lincolnshire in the civil wars of the 1640s was determined more by geographical location than by political adherence, for there was no stronghold in the county decisively committed to one side or the other. Lincolnshire lay within a sphere of parliamentary influence, surrounded by supporters of parliament in East Anglia, south Yorkshire and Nottingham. But at the heart of this region was the royalist fortress of Newark: so strongly partisan were the men of Newark that they even rejected an order from the king himself to surrender. Controlling the crossing of the Trent, it kept the road to London open for the king's army and barred the movement of parliamentary troops from East Anglia into the north.

Red Hall, Bourne

The nature of the wars was less one of set battles than of minor skirmishes focussed on the estates of gentry who raised money and troops for one side or the other and fortified their houses against the bands of soldiers who tried to enforce obedience to king or parliament. Newark's role was to rally the pockets of king's supporters in the region and to harass the enemy; it was the nerve centre of loyalist resistance at Belvoir (the earl of Rutland), at Welbeck, Shelford and Wiverton in Nottinghamshire and the Brownlow residence at Belton by Grantham.

Within the county, opinions were divided. More people seem to have adhered to parliament than to the king, but the men of Lincolnshire were more concerned with local issues, and the king could count on support from those who felt they had most to gain in their local controversies from the royalists. There were a few stable allegiances; even in the Fens where parliament's chief strength lay, Crowland persistently supported the king.

The first civil war

When trouble broke out in 1642, rival emergency administrations were appointed in the county. The king chose Robert Bertie, Lord Willoughby d'Eresby (from 1627 first earl of Lindsey) as lord lieutenant for Lincolnshire, while parliament turned to Lord Willoughby of Parham. Commissioners were sent to control the militia and raise troops – M.P.s for parliament and loyal J.P.s for the king. On the whole parliament won this first round. There was some opposition; one man pinned up a bill from the king forbidding the muster of troops on the door of the inn where Lord Willoughby was staying. But although the king paid a visit to Lincoln in July 1642 amid scenes of enthusiasm, Lindsey's

69

authority was ineffective, and few troops were raised for the crown (one Boston woman sent to the earl one of her husband's toes, deliberately cut off so that he should not be drafted into the king's army). Parliamentary supporters continued to recruit and train soldiers in the county.

When war broke out, parliament fortified Lincoln city and castle and held the county against the king. Resistance to parliament was seen early in 1643 at Crowland where the inhabitants, armed with 'fennish weapons' of scythes and pitchforks and led by their vicar, held out for four months behind specially made defences. Crowland lay on one of the main routes across the Fens especially important to the parliamentary forces, and it took an army under Oliver Cromwell to suppress this royalist revolt.

Three-way bridge, Crowland

Cromwell went on to attack Newark. An attempt to capture this town in February 1643 had merely resulted in a series of counter-attacks from Newark which had strengthened Crowland's resistance and increased the king's influence in places like Grantham and Stamford. Royalist troops rode freely throughout south Lincolnshire and won skirmishes against Lord Willoughby's forces on the heath between Ancaster and Grantham. To meet this menace, Cromwell marched north in April 1643 with his New Model Army; but he had little more success and his withdrawal led to further raids from the fortress, this time towards Lincoln and Louth.

Cromwell's failure enabled the royalists to defeat Sir Thomas Fairfax, parliament's commander in Yorkshire. This was the king's opportunity; with Cromwell falling back into East Anglia, the road to London lay open. The earl of Newcastle led the king's army into the county. He stopped to take Gainsborough, a crucial crossing point on the Trent which still held out for parliament. Cromwell saw a chance of forcing the king's army into battle, but although he won an engagement at Lea, he was unable to drive off the royalist forces and the town fell to Newcastle. This severe setback to parliament's interests caused Willoughby to withdraw from Lincoln to Boston, Cromwell from Stamford to Peterborough. A new front line was drawn across Lincolnshire. King's Lynn declared for the king and had to be captured by the earl of Manchester at the head of parliament's Eastern Association troops.

All was thus poised for a final confrontation in September 1643. But the royalists delayed, too unsure of their position to make a decisive move. Like the parliamentary forces, they had made themselves unpopular by plundering Gainsborough, Lincoln and other centres. More important they feared to leave the unconquered stronghold of Hull behind them, even though Grimsby was loyalist. Cromwell and Willoughby managed to get some troops out of Hull by sea and concentrate them at Lynn, and from there Manchester advanced to Boston, Bolingbroke castle which he captured and Horncastle; at Winceby the battle which the parliamentary army was seeking was fought (11 October 1643) and the royalists were defeated. Newcastle withdrew into Yorkshire and the county reverted to parliamentary control. As a contemporary writer put

70

it, the parliamentary gentry driven from their lands by the king's army were 'relincolnshired again'. With their troops reorganised, their finances once more healthy and their new allies the Scots on the march, parliament hoped for a swift and final victory. The king sought help from the Danes, but parliament controlled the sea and prevented the Danish forces from landing in Lincolnshire.

Local loyalties

This was nearly the end of the war in the county. An attempt to capture Newark in March 1644 was foiled by Prince Rupert and royalist interests in the county revived; the parliamentary fortifications at Gainsborough and Lincoln were dismantled and their garrisons at Sleaford and Crowland were thrown out. But Manchester and Cromwell advanced through the area again, plundering and destroying religious monuments; at Lincoln where Manchester's siege in June 1645 provoked a good deal of resistance, the cathedral suffered damage, and at Crowland the town and monastic ruins were enthusiastically sacked, the last of the medieval glass being destroyed. The parliamentary troops passed into Yorkshire, crossing the Trent at Gainsborough, and at Marston Moor the royalists were heavily beaten. From there, the war passed into the west.

Cromwell was prevented from besieging Newark by disputes between the commanders. During 1645, raids from the castle continued. Torksey House and Hougham House, held by parliamentary garrisons, were attacked, and the small pockets of royalists at Stamford and Crowland encouraged. But early in 1646 the Scots invested Newark and in May the king surrendered; further resistance to parliament in the name of the king was useless.

But the parliamentarians in Lincolnshire were divided amongst themselves. Colonel Edward King of Ashby de la Launde, supported by Manchester, ousted Lord Willoughby of Parham from his leadership of parliament's interests; King was made governor of Holland and Boston and later of Lincoln, but his exercise of power made him unpopular. Deprived of office he became the focus of opposition to the parliamentary committee headed by Thomas Hatcher of Careby in 1646. The royalists under Monckton tried to build on this disagreement when the second civil war broke out, but apart from a few skirmishes around Belvoir in 1648, Lincolnshire took no action to aid the king.

But equally there was not much support for the army. The men of Lincolnshire were more interested in local issues. The inhabitants of Sleaford, for instance, took the opportunity to pay off old scores against Sir Robert Carr, and Crowland waged war against Spalding and other fenland settlements. Some, like John Becke, mayor of Lincoln, defended local interests against both sides; the men of Axholme flooded the Isle against the king's army, but they also resisted Cromwell's parliament when it ordered them to return the lands they had re-appropriated.

At the heart of these struggles lay hostility to central control over the county. Sir John Wray of Glentworth and Ashby, M.P. had led opposi-

Sir John Smith, early American colonist

71

tion to Westminster's increasing interference since at least 1627 on issues such as ship money, the county militia and drainage. He supported the House of Commons and those 'numerous godly precious people' the commoners, in their resistance to royal schemes to drain the Isle of Axholme, but the violence which accompanied this and other protests against enclosure made many gentry look to the king to provide strong government. By 1648 parliament turned against the commoners, and thus, when Col. Rossiter came to raise troops for parliament, he found his task more difficult than in earlier years.

It was the riots in 1649-50 which led the Levellers Lilburne and Wildman to move into Axholme in an attempt to take over the leadership of a promising revolutionary movement. But they failed – perhaps because they bought freehold land for themselves, perhaps because they were outsiders, or perhaps because in the end Lincolnshire was not a centre of radicalism. The arguments and ideologies of the Levellers did not match the burning questions of the inhabitants of Axholme. For the men of Lincolnshire, 'their war was with enclosure, loss of common rights and enforced change rather than with King or Parliament'; 'they would never have taken Arms for the Parliament, but that they intended thereby to have power in their hands to destroy the Draining and Improvements and lay all waste again to their Common'.

Religious persuasions

Religion seems to have played relatively little part in the conflict in Lincolnshire. Popular Catholicism had largely died out except amongst a few gentry and landed families. Puritanism was mostly within the established church, particularly in the towns where preachers like John Cotton at Boston and John Vicars at Stamford held sway. No less than 14 puritan 'lecturers' preached in Grantham church, and they led the vocal opposition when the vicar of Grantham moved the altar from the centre of the chancel to the east end of his church. Separatist congregations were rare; an Anabaptist group existed in Axholme in 1626-34, and two preachers 'led out' congregations, John Smith from Lincoln to Gainsborough and John Robinson to Scrooby in Nottinghamshire nearby. Both of these groups soon left for Holland, some of them who had followed Robinson proceeding to America as the 'Pilgrim Fathers'.

Separatist congregations spread quickly during the Commonwealth and Protectorate, mainly in Axholme, the Marsh and the Fens. Thomas Grantham founded a Baptist church in Boston in the 1640s, and the Quakers led by John Whitehead flourished in several centres, notably Gainsborough and Brant Broughton. More extreme sects like the Manifestarians made their appearance in the Fens. But they were still few, no more than three per cent of the population and even at their densest probably still only some six per cent. The majority of laity and clergy remained faithful to the Elizabethan settlement, like Robert Sanderson of Boothby Pagnell, imprisoned for his loyalty to the Prayer Book and later rewarded by becoming bishop of Lincoln. Parliament ejected more than 90 Lincolnshire clergy from their livings during the Interregnum – all the incumbents of Stamford were removed between 1645 and 1649; and at the Restoration in 1660, some 60 puritan clergy were in their turn ejected.

Economic pressures

Life was perhaps less affected by the 'troubles' than by plagues (as in 1603) and famine (1623) which afflicted Lincolnshire in the early 17th century. The trends set at the end of the previous century continued. Population increased, especially in the Fens and in the towns. The number of urban centres in the county continued to grow, and places like Pinchbeck in the Fens flourished for a time. The results of the garrisoning and besieging of the towns have not yet been worked out in detail but places like Stamford and Gainsborough clearly suffered. There were other short-term effects of the disturbances: Parliament confiscated the property of royalists and imposed heavy fines for their recovery. The pre-civil war drainage schemes were abandoned and the commoners reoccupied the land. But the growth of population and continuation of inflation increased pressure on the wasteland. Enclosure and drainage schemes were now intended more to accommodate new people than to dispossess common right holders. In some places, scattered strips were consolidated into farms, and increasingly land was let out on long leases. The gentry now drew more of their wealth from the profits of farming and reinvested it not just in more land but in industrial and exploitative enterprises outside the county. A new elite of tenant farmers was being created, men who exercised leadership in their communities, serving as parish officers in the new pattern of local government devised and directed by central government.

County and court

The growth of central control over the political and administrative life of the regions was the main focus of political life at the end of the century. Up to about 1660, M.P.s for the county and towns reflected local opinion in the councils of the nation. Such opinion could on occasion be divided: on the death of Cromwell, three Lincolnshire M.P.s represented different views of the way to be taken. John Weaver of Stamford urged a return to a republic, William Ellis of Grantham sought a renewal of the Protectorate and Col Edward Rossiter of Somerby, a county M.P. argued for a restoration of Charles II, despite his former parliamentary allegiance. On the whole Lincolnshire supported the restoration of the monarchy; indeed a plot was laid for a rising in the county on behalf of Charles, but it never materialised.

Fydell House, Boston

Perhaps this is the reason why Lincolnshire was treated relatively moderately after 1660. Persecution of dissenting groups was on the whole light; there was more interest in the public quarrel between the Baptists and the Quakers in Axholme. But here as elsewhere, the towns lost their charters to the crown, and the civil courts waged war against the church courts. As central control over the regions grew, the role of the king's justices and officials changed. They were chosen more to represent central government's interests in the shire than to reflect the county's concerns to central government. And for this purpose the court sought to secure amenable M.P.s

And it was this which accounts for the contests that the shires saw in the late 17th century. Sir Robert Carr of Sleaford and Sir Christopher Hussey in the 1660s successfully resisted the reinstatement of courtiers in the drainage schemes in Lindsey, despite royal support. From 1676, Robert Bertie third earl of Lindsey led the 'court' party, opposed by Carr, Sir Thomas Meres of Scotton and Sir John Monson of Carlton. Gradually Carr emerged as the leader of the 'county' faction and from 1679, after the Popish plot of Titus Oates, began to build up a party for himself. Initially both Carr and the earl of Lindsey were opposed to the radical tendencies of the 'whigs', but later Carr's hostility to Lindsey at parliamentary elections and by-elections led him to be seen as the leader of the whigs in the county.

Carr died in 1682 and the 'tories' under Lindsey dominated Lincoln-shire. In 1685 when the Monmouth rebellion broke out, there was no support for the rising in the county, but Lindsey took the opportunity to imprison some of his opponents. But in 1688 when William of Orange invaded, Lindsey's heir Lord Willoughby seized York for William while Lindsey did nothing despite the riots which broke out in several places, notably Axholme. Some old tories were never reconciled to the change of dynasty – the Monsons, Bolles and Oldfields, for example – and party rivalry remained intense; but the majority of the Lincolnshire establishment supported the Orange and later the Hanoverian court and thus helped to undermine the county's regional identity and inde-pendence.

Sir John Franklin, the explorer

IX Drainage

The men who in December 1642 opened the newly made sluice gates and flooded large areas of the Isle of Axholme, preventing the king's army from passing, were directing their hostility both against the drainers, the Dutch Cornelius Vermuyden and his fellow undertakers, and against the king who had given them their commission. Opposition to drainage, and with it enclosure, the passing of common land into private ownership, more than religion or politics motivated their actions; the men of Axholme were in danger of losing their livelihood.

Wrawby post mill

Drainage was the most conspicuous aspect of the trend to improve Lincolnshire's wastelands. The dry heathlands and the sandy areas near Scunthorpe and on the west face of the Wolds were improved rather later, but the wetlands of Marsh, clay vales and Fens were a more urgent problem; a third of the county's land surface lay at or below sea level.

The lands

One third of the English Fens lay in Lincolnshire around the Wash. Five major rivers met here, the Witham, Glen, Welland, Nene and Ouse, and the morass had been built up by inundation from the sea, freshwater floods off the land and the deposit of silt. At the point where the rivers met the sea, a ridge had been built up, marked by a line of villages each with its medieval stone church as at Algarkirk or Gedney. At its nearest point (Donington) where the ridge was no more than five miles from the Kesteven heathlands, a road developed from prehistoric times. To the east of this ridge lay the salt marshes, rich grazing land; to the west lay the inner fens, freshwater peat marshes, most difficult of all to drain. As the sea was pushed back by sea walls, the rivers had to flow longer distances as well as pass through the silt belt; the fall was so little that the slow flow of the water in the rivers meant that the channels were frequently blocked.

Like the Fens, the Marsh between the Wolds and sea fell into two parts, the inner freshwater marshes and the narrower outer salt marshes. The lower Witham valley was a natural extension to the Fens and probably the worst of all the flooded lands of the county, but the Ancholme, Trent and upper Witham valleys and Axholme were almost as bad. All these lands had their own way of life, social structure and agricultural practices (like 'warping' on the lower Trent, systematic flooding to secure a deposit of river silt on the land); and they have

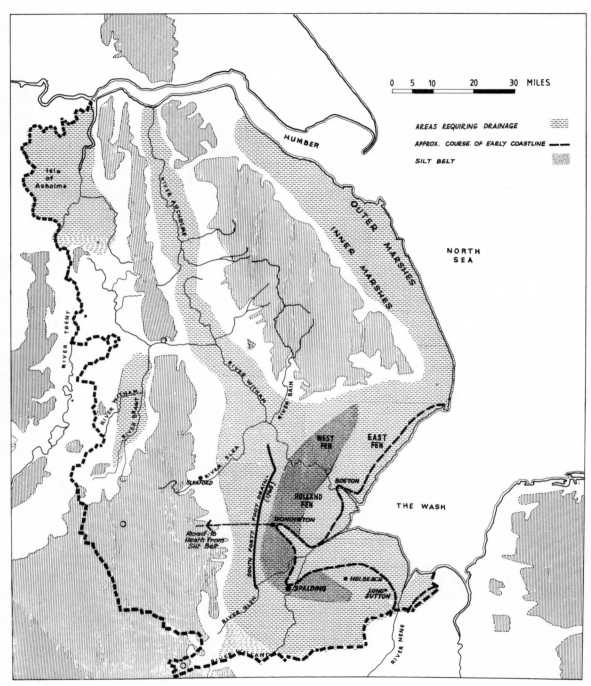

Map legend:

0 5 10 20 30 MILES

AREAS REQUIRING DRAINAGE
APPROX. COURSE OF EARLY COASTLINE
SILT BELT

HUMBER

NORTH SEA

Isle of Axholme

RIVER TRENT

OUTER MARSHES

INNER MARSHES

RIVER WITHAM

RIVER BRANT

RIVER BAIN

WEST FEN

EAST FEN

SLEAFORD

RIVER SLEA

BOSTON

HOLLAND FEN

THE WASH

BONINGTON

SOUTH FORTY FOOT (1635)

Road to Heath from Silt Belt

HOLBEACH

SPALDING

LONG SUTTON

RIVER GLEN

RIVER WELLAND

RIVER NENE

17. Drainage in Lincolnshire.

given Lincolnshire its reputation as 'a region of fertility without beauty' – Drayton's 'foule and woosie Marsh' was 'rich in Corne and Pastures'.

The inhabitants of this 'vast and queachy soil with hosts of wallowing waves' were equally 'rude, uncivil and envious to all others whom they call Uplandmen . . . very poor, lazy, given to much fishing and idleness'. The seasonal activities of the fenland exploiters were seen by others as idleness leading to economic and cultural poverty; and their hostility to drainage was fear that 'their condition should be worse, which truly was impossible'.

They had had a hard struggle over many centuries to occupy these lands. The gains made by the Romans were wiped out in the Anglo-Saxon period, and the early medieval years saw the lands at their most underdeveloped since prehistoric times, the home of hermits, refugees and terrorist bands. The subsequent colonisation and exploitation of the area passed through four main phases, each associated with new technology, dyking, new cuts, windmills and power pumps.

Phase I: Commissions of Sewers

The Middle Ages saw both the erosion of the south Yorkshire and Lincolnshire coastline which deposited sand and silt in the Humber and Wash, and at the same time bursts of frequent and severe floods, especially in 1176-8, 1248-88, 1323-35 and 1404-30. The main enemy was the sea; catchment drains and sea walls were built, co-operative ventures by whole villages. Central government began to encourage and regulate this work, and from 1258 local gentry were appointed to Commissions of Sewers (with new powers from 1427) to keep the channels clear and the banks repaired. But success was limited; local rivalries over grazing rights and boundaries, especially in the Deeping area, leading to law suits and violence, and further floods and silting of the channels combined to undo much of this work.

Alford Mill

The disastrous floods of the 16th century which destroyed whole settlements (Skegness 1526, Mablethorpe 1540s, and especially 1571 immortalised by Jean Ingelow's *High Tide on the Coast of Lincolnshire*) led to some new schemes – sea walls in the Marsh (1568), the Maud Foster Drain, the Welland Act (1570) and new drains around the Deepings, Spalding and Pinchbeck (1590s); while in 1529 the 29 parishes with grazing in East, West and Wildmore Fens drew up rules to avoid disputes over common rights.

Phase II: New cuts

Such work called for more capital and more advanced technology than was available locally, and the king, in his need to raise funds independently of parliament, stepped in. He commissioned the work, raised the money needed from 'participants' (groups of courtiers, merchants, nobility and local gentry) and hired Vermuyden and his skilled engineers. The technique of cutting new short straight channels, thus increasing the

77

*Sibsey
Trader
mill*

flow of water and keeping the rivers from silting up was first tried by the earl of Bedford in the Cambridgeshire Fens. In Lincolnshire work began in Axholme, 1626-36; 60,000 acres were put under contract to the Dutch drainage experts, 40,000 acres to go to the king and the rest to be retained for their labours. The results were impressive – new land was cultivated, Dutch and French Huguenots settled at Sandtoft, industries sprang up and some workers' wages were doubled. But many people lost their land and riots broke out. Both king and parliament earned the hostility of the dispossessed Islanders and the Levellers joined in; most of the work was undone in the 1640s and 1650s.

Elsewhere in Lincolnshire the drainage schemes were privately rather than government inspired, undertaken by local landowners and courtiers. In 1610 the earl of Exeter started work on 30,000 acres between Deeping and Spalding but floods and malicious activity caused the scheme to be abandoned (1631) and Bedford added this region to his Great Level drainage scheme in 1638. Sir John Monson drained 18,000 acres in the Ancholme valley (1634), Sir Anthony Meres began work in the north Fens (1631-4), and part of the southern Fens (Tydd) were drained in 1632. The courtier family Killigrew, father and son, commenced the drainage and enclosure of 40,000 acres in East, West and Wildmore Fens from 1635, and the earl of Lindsey attacked the Lindsey levels in 1635-9 and the Holland Fens 1635-8.

All this activity faced bitter opposition from the small freeholders and tenant farmers who had moved into the fens in large numbers in the 17th century, attracted by the availability of land. They relied heavily on pastures for their living, and the drainage schemes made pastures increasingly scarce. The opponents argued that drainage was not necessary for the profitable exploitation of the region. The demand for the produce of the fens was increasing – fish for manure, reeds for thatching and furniture, peat for fuel, ash and willow, cranberries, wild fowl; grazing land supported cattle, sheep, hogs, geese (for food, down and quills) and horses (Wildmore Fen and Boston).

A large population thus lived a way of life alien to those outside the region, 'a kind of predatory life . . . ; a life of laziness is generally preferred . . . fishing and shooting and catching wild fowl may be called amusement rather than labour'. Petitions in support of the traditional shepherding in summer and fowling and fishing in winter were being presented to the drainage commissioners as late as 1784. It was urged that the new arable crops were alien, that drainage and intensive cultivation would exhaust the soil, that floods kept the land fertile, that drainage only moved the floods to another place (it was alleged that the drainage had caused, not alleviated, floods in 1639-40).

The commoners of the fens and nearby upland villages which had rights in the fens combined, subscribed to a common purse, went to law and on occasion took direct action, breaking drains and banks. Lawlessness was widespread throughout the fenland areas and this was a further motivation for drainage: the fenmen, wrote an undertaker, lived

78

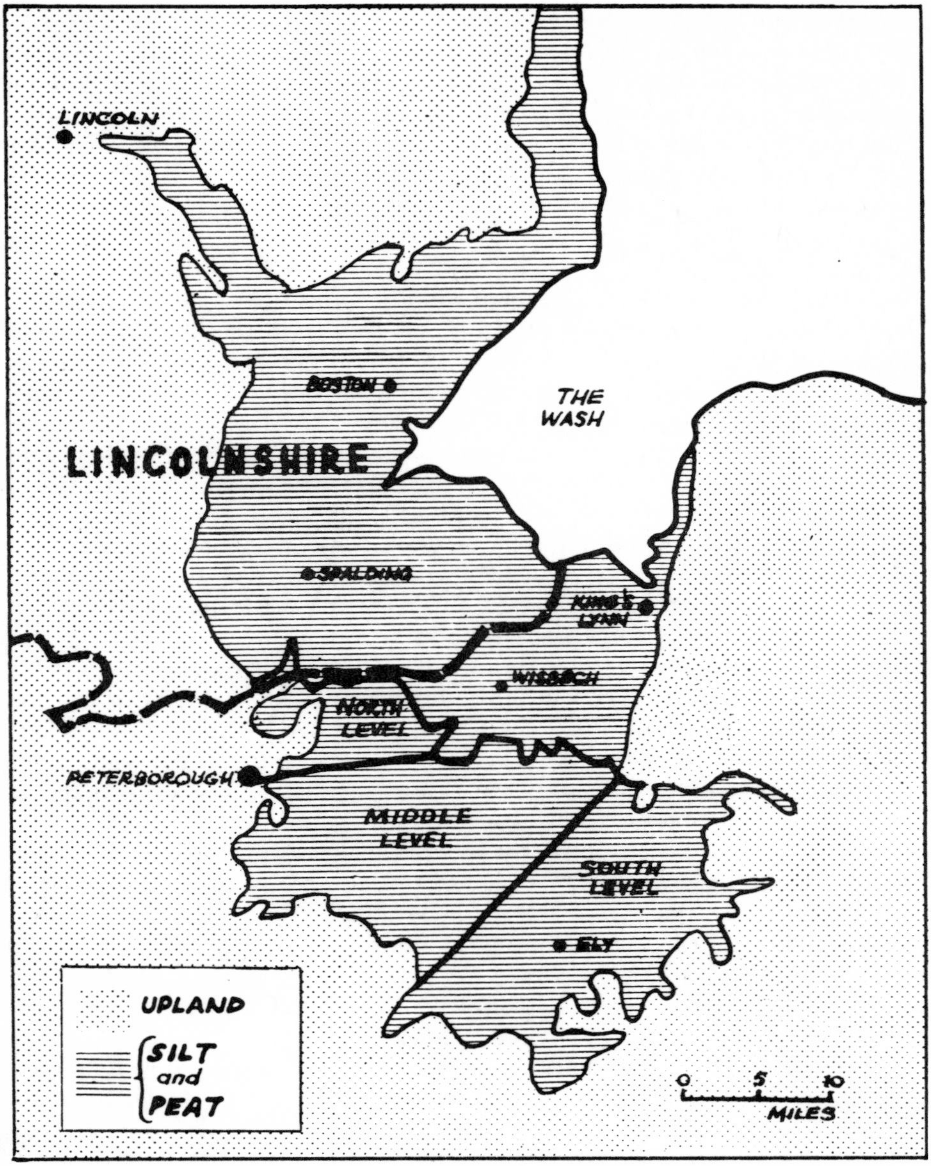
LINCOLN
BOSTON
THE WASH
LINCOLNSHIRE
SPALDING
KING'S LYNN
WISBECH
NORTH LEVEL
PETERBOROUGH
MIDDLE LEVEL
SOUTH LEVEL
ELY
UPLAND
SILT and PEAT
0 5 10
MILES

18. The English Fenlands.

'like the Aborigines of North America, a kind of lawless life, almost in a state of nature, and their ideas, wild as their native Fens . . . not very easily subjected to reason or control'. Riots broke out in Axholme (1627-34), in East, West and Wildmore Fens (1635-41) and in the Holland Fens (1638-40). Although damage was usually limited and personal injury small, the resistance was persistent and in the end won; by 1649 all the early schemes had been undone. The Restoration saw two half-hearted revivals, in the Ancholme valley and in the Deeping Fen, but attempts to collect drainage taxes provoked further riots and nothing more was done until the 18th century. The fens reverted to their earlier way of life; instead of corn 'a great number of fat oxen and sheep are weekly sent to London in droves . . . great plenty and variety of fowl and fish are usually taken in decoys and sent to London' (1696).

Phase III: Windmills

Pasture had won; and as population grew and the economy of eastern and midland England expanded, the enclosures of the upland parishes of Lincolnshire for arable created an increased demand for grazing land. Attention thus turned to the inner fens rather than to more sea walls reclaiming the outer salt fens and marshes. There were however major problems. The earlier drainage had caused the peat to shrink so that the inner fens were now lower than the outer fens, lower than the rivers that drained them; and the land was still sinking in relation to the sea, so that the flow of water in the rivers and drainage channels slowed down still further. The rivers had to be raised to cross the silt belt and flow to the now distant sea. Floods, sheep rot and cattle disease, prevalent in the 1730s and 1740s, called for action.

Heckington mill

The answer was found in the windmill, so admired by Defoe in his visit to Lincolnshire, and in the sluice gate. The process this time was largely by Act of Parliament and Drainage Boards. The earliest windmills used to pump water off the land were in the Deeping Fens (1729) but the main onslaught came later. Drainage was now linked to schemes for turnpike roads, enclosure and canals; some parishes sold off undrained areas to help pay for the enclosing of their arable open fields. In 1762 the Witham Act led to the first really successful attempt to drain this valley; in 1765 the new Black Sluice Drainage Board tackled the area between Boston and Bourne, and severe floods in 1763 led to the navigable South Forty Foot drain (1767). More work on the lower Witham (1772-6) was followed by an Act to drain the south Holland Fens near Sutton Bridge (1792).

The costs were high (some £400,000 to drain the north Holland Fens), raised by loans and rates on the occupiers of the new lands, but the profits were great. Arthur Young in 1799 reported that rough grazing land had now become profitable, yielding 11s or even 17s rent per acre instead of 1s 6d: 'this vast work is effected by a moderate embankment and the erection of windmills for throwing out the superfluous water'. Large numbers of windmills were needed – 63 along the South Forty Foot Drain.

There were riots in Holland Fen between 1768 and 1773, and murder, hamstringing and stack burning elsewhere, but this opposition died out; when the last undrained lands, East, West and Wildmore Fens between Boston and the Wolds were improved, 1801-20, the sub-division and

80

alienation of the parochial allotments (land given to upland parishes like Horncastle as compensation for the loss of fenland grazing rights), although bitterly resented, did not lead to violence.

By the 1820s, the main drainage lines had been laid out. Much of the new lands (more than a third in the Lindsey Fen) was sold to pay the costs of drainage and enclosure or for the endowment of churches to serve new settlements like Holbeach St Matthew or Holbeach St Mark. Farms were laid out in the reclaimed lands with mathematical precision as at Gedney. The Act of 1812 dealing with East, West and Wildmore Fens resulted in seven new settlements with exotic names like Eastville, Midville, Frithville and Langrickville, while elsewhere names like New York appeared in Lincolnshire.

Phase IV: Engines

But still more effective technology was needed to stop the flooding. In 1799 pamphlets protested that 'many hundred acres of the harvest were reaped by men in boats [while others] stodd up to their waists in water' and cut off the heads of corn which showed above the surface. Steam pumps were first used for drainage in place of windmills in the southern fens (Pode Hole near Spalding 1825) and spread northwards. They were in use in the Witham Fen in the 1820s and in the Holland Fen 1848-9. Again there was opposition; it took the severe floods of 1866 to persuade the northern fenlanders to install the machinery at Lode Bank. But they were effective. Virtually no new drainage work was necessary; some attention was given to the outfalls of the rivers in the 1880s, and sea marshes were reclaimed at the mouths of the Witham and Welland. From the 1940s, steam pumps have been replaced by diesel or electric pumping stations. The inundation of 1953 shows that the danger is still there, and schemes to turn the Wash into a freshwater reservoir are usually linked with co-ordinated drainage plans for the whole of the English Fens.

The main battles were fought and won; and the changes were dramatic. Although possessed of 'a climate not salubrious to the human constitution', the region became 'one of the richest tracts in the kingdom . . . the population has grown in numbers, in health and in comfort . . . the haunts of pike and wild fowl have become the habitation of industrious farmers and husbandmen' (Arthur Young, 1813). Steam packets and other traffic passed along the rivers and drains. Despite the 'quaking peat', a hazard to house builder and railway engineer alike, new farms were erected often dated by their names (Crimea Farm, etc), trees were planted for shelter, and grazing lands became arable. Cobbett in the 1830s still saw pastures: 'land covered with beautiful grass, with sheep lying about upon it as fat as hogs . . . earth without a stone as big as a pin's head; grass as thick as it can grow in the ground; immense bowling greens separated by ditches'. But mostly the farmers turned to arable — oats, cole-seed in the northern fens, hemp, flax, potatoes and beans in Axholme, and even woad, opium and tobacco were tried.

Pode Hole pumping station

81

X Agriculture and Society 1750-1850

The years 1750-1850 saw some of the most striking changes in Lincolnshire's history. This was the age of turnpike roads, canals and the first railways; of Methodism; of the conversion of towns like Lincoln and Boston into industrial centres. But it was in agriculture that the greatest changes took place, transforming the landscape until the county emerged 'first in rank among the English counties for agricultural development'. Population grew rapidly;it was probably at its highest rate between 1800 and 1850 when it doubled from 200,000 to just over 400,000. The Fens with its common rights, drainage and small farms, and the Kesteven uplands seem to have absorbed most of this increase. Agriculture responded by increasing the amount of land available for cultivation and then by exploiting new agricultural techniques and inceasing output.

Bust of George III

Common lands and enclosure

Lincolnshire had for many centuries been primarily a pastoral area, producing meat and wool on its common grazing lands; cattle from Scotland, fattened on the marshes and fens, went to London in droves each week. Enclosures of these commons, either for permanent grass or to grow fodder crops for winter, had proceeded until by 1600 about a quarter of the county's open lands had been enclosed, and another quarter went between 1600 and 1750. It seems to have been the heavy wet soils of the clay vales, more suited to cattle than to corn, which felt this process most.

Common land was of three kinds – the wetlands of fen and marshes, the heathlands, and the cultivated open fields. The latter were in most cases open at some time of the year to grazing in common, and a mixed economy flourished: Billingborough in 1739 was

> environ'd with fertile fields and pleasant meadows ... The fields are commonly sown with wheat, barley, peas and beans, all which they bear very good . the fields have a good sort of sheep on them ... but sometimes they are subject to take the rott ... Horses thrive and grow fatt in the fenn, of which they have plenty. Ash and willow grow plentifully, but want more planters.

But the need to consolidate scattered holdings into 'profitable farms [by which] a great produce is created, cattle and sheep increased and the poor employed' grew as time went on.

The upland scrub 'covered with heath, gorse and yielding little or no

82

produce' (Arthur Young, 1799) and the sandy soils 'like the deserts of Egypt and Arabie' (de la Pryme, 1695) were used less. Apart from sheep and cattle, there were rabbits. Warrens of 3-4000 acres (Blankney, Thoresway) and 1000 acres (Withcall near Louth) were the basis of a fur industry: 'it is said that more hands are employed here [Brigg] in dressing rabbit skins than in any other town in the kingdom'. The steep hillsides and wastelands were fenced, guarded against poachers and in places cultivated in rotation – corn, turnips and pasture grass. But rabbits were regarded as 'nuisances' and warrens 'a melancholy scene, more of desolation than culture'.

Swallow Farm

Warrens, wetlands, wastelands, common lands, open fields all became subject to clearance and cultivation, sometimes by agreement between villagers and landlords, sometimes by Acts of Parliament. Over 360 Enclosure Acts were passed for Lincolnshire, half of them between 1750 and 1780, and a further 165 after 1800. The Wolds and Heath, clay vales and some of the fens were enclosed mostly between 1760 and 1780, the Marsh and other areas between 1790 and 1820. By 1815 all the open fields in south Lincolnshire except Stamford had gone and most of the wastes had been brought into cultivation.

Sleaford is a good example of this process. Here two parishes, New Sleaford with Holdingham and Old Sleaford with Quarrington, were enclosed by an Act of 1794. Each parish had its own system, three great fields. There were some 'old enclosures', small fields so long enclosed that no one knew if they had ever been part of the open fields or not. Several persons in the town of Sleaford (only one of them a farmer) had rights of grazing on the fens and heathlands. The earl of Bristol (also bishop of Derry) owned most of the land in both parishes and managed his estate through Edward Waterson, vicar of Sleaford and rector of Quarrington, as well as holder of other lucrative offices and sinecures.

Lord Bristol got the Act passed. Commissioners were appointed, Stanley Marshall, a grazier from Frieston in Holland with experience of drainage, John Parkinson of Asgarby, land agent of Sir Joseph Banks of Revesby and an experienced enclosure commissioner, and Anthony Peacock of South Kyme, a landowner and deputy lieutenant for the county. The solicitor Benjamin Handley of Sleaford was clerk to the commissioners. There were many men of this type constantly involved in improvement schemes, like John Cragg of Threekingham and Benjamin Smith of Horbling, clerks to navigation companies, turnpike trusts, commissioners of sewers and of enclosure, and J.P.s.

Heath Farm, North Ranceby

Enclosure was expensive and landlords invested heavily in their estates. The costs of the Act, the expenses of commissioners and surveyors and the new roads and fences were met by the proprietors at anything between 17s and 40s per acre; in cases of exceptional difficulty, when the process took as long as 20 or 30 years to complete, costs could be £7 or even £8 per acre. The Sleaford enclosure cost some £4000; at Barrow (1797-1803) more than £15,000 was paid, and at North Kelsey, a small enclosure which took from 1813 to 1840 to complete, costs were

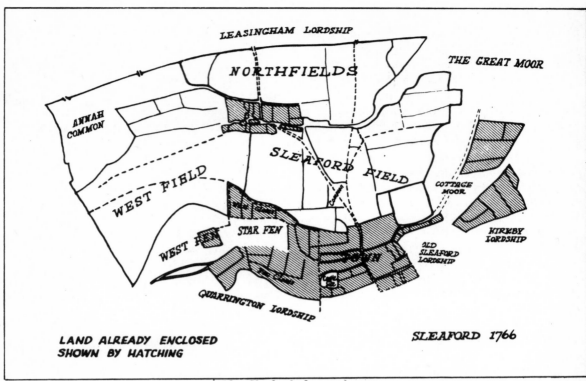

LEASINGHAM LORDSHIP

THE GREAT MOOR

NORTHFIELDS

ANNAH COMMON

SLEAFORD FIELD

WEST FIELD

COTTAGE MOOR

KIRKBY LORDSHIP

STAR FEN

WEST FEN

OLD SLEAFORD LORDSHIP

QUARRINGTON LORDSHIP

LAND ALREADY ENCLOSED
SHOWN BY HATCHING

SLEAFORD 1766

19. Sleaford after enclosure.

RIVER SLEA

LAND ALREADY ENCLOSED IN 1766
SHOWN BY HATCHING (See FIGURE 8)

SLEAFORD 1960

84

£12,500. Banks came to the rescue; every main market town had its own bank like the Sleaford Bank established by Peacock and Handley in 1792 which made great profits from schemes like the Slea Navigation, the Deeping Fen enclosure and the Witham improvement. But if the costs of enclosure, building new farmhouses and stocking the farms were high, so were the profits: lord Bristol's rents rose by £1600 p.a., while at Rauceby nearby the value of the vicarage rose from £30 p.a. before enclosure to £165 p.a.

Out of the six fields, the commons and fens surrounding Sleaford, the commissioners made compact new farms with smaller fields surrounded by hedges. New farmhouses were built. The psychological impact of this reallocation must have been enormous. Sometimes long discussions preceded enclosure; at Ulceby in north Lindsey enclosure was planned five times between 1801 and 1818 and finally agreed in 1823. New farming meant new practices. In the Trent valley warping gave way to the use of marl and manure. Selective breeding of cattle and sheep was now possible. In some areas like Axholme there was an increase in arable; barley was grown on the enclosed heathlands and grain production began to replace the fat beef and mutton which had been the county's main produce in the 18th century. The ploughing of land quickened during the Napoleonic Wars (1793-1815) when corn prices were high but after the wars some of this land reverted to pasture. New crops like cole-seed and turnips were grown and there was an increase in oats, much of it for fodder; in many parts of Lincolnshire the emphasis remained on cattle and sheep.

Improvements

Lincolnshire produced no great agricultural experimenter of the standing of Coke of Norfolk or Robert Bakewell of Leicestershire. Major Cartwright established a Model Farm at Brothertoft and experimented with woad. Sir Joseph Banks of Revesby was a key figure, President of the Royal Society and patron of Cook, supporter of drainage, turnpikes and canals in the county. The most important improvers were perhaps Charles Chaplin at Blankney, Christopher Turner at Paunton and especially the lords Yarborough, father and son, of Brocklesby; they improved their estates, planted trees, built farmhouses and cottages, introduced a wider rotation of crops. Lord Willoughby d'Eresby at Edenham used new machinery like the steam plough which he exhibited at the 1851 Great Exhibition.

Arch commemorating Lord Yarborough, Brocklesby

The pattern of landlordship in the county still needs further investigation. Owners with more than 3000 acres seem to have been congregated in Kesteven and on the Wolds; the Kesteven landlords formed part of an East Midlands agricultural community in a region bounded by Grantham, Stamford and Leicester, and several were non-resident. Those on the Wolds were fewer and tended to reside on their estates. Here the more numerous gentry with 300-3000 acres consolidated their hold on the economy and social life of the area. The smaller owners with less than 300 acres predominated in the drained lands of Axholme and the Fens. This pattern grew stronger as time passed; in Kesteven the gentry seem to have driven out the smaller holders, while in the Marsh and Fens the break-up of estates by absentee landlords led to an increase in the number of smaller owners.

The predominance of landlords (half of Lincolnshire's soil was owned by holders of 1000 acres or more) led to the emergence of the substantial tenant farmer, the most typical character of the county's social structure at this period. Sometimes radical in a polite sort of way, like the Methodist Cornelius Stovin, but mostly conservative, they were often indistinguishable from many of the gentry farmer owners like Robert Carr Brackenbury. Fiercely possessive of their lands, although rented, it was these who experimented with new agricultural practices. The increase in productivity and profits (enclosed parishes produced more wheat and much more oats and barley per acre than parishes still open) at first went to benefit the landlord but later, especially after 1825 when rents were lowered 'on Account of the Depression in value of Agricultural Produce', the tenants took the lion's share. Those who did not buy their own farms at this time still invested large sums in their holdings. They were protected by 'tenant-right', or Lincolnshire Custom, which grew up in the early 19th century, by which a tenant leaving his land received payments for improvements done. They thus put in tile drains, spread lime, chalk, marl and fertilisers like bone and guano, and grew new crops.

The Orangery, Holywell

Regional differences became less marked and the county's economy became even more closely interwoven and interdependent. The towns relied for their industry and markets on the farms; upland farmers needed lowland pastures and often held lands far from their home farm. The Marsh provides an example of this network; some of the rich pastures used for fattening and breeding sheep and cattle were held by marshland graziers who bought stock from upland farmers and sold them in the markets of London and elsewhere, but in other parts the upland farmers drove out the graziers, buying up holdings and exploiting them directly, 'for their own lands were too poor to fatt' their own stock. There are thus in many parts of the Marsh few large houses and plantations, signs of the wealthy resident farmer-gentleman.

The county was still noted for its stock. Arthur Young commented on the rich cattle (1799), and in 1800 the pastures were 'the glory of Lincolnshire'. At the end of the 18th century Thomas Turnell of Reasby near Lincoln established the forerunner of the Lincoln Red Shorthorn which William Torr of Aylesby made famous in the 1840s. Torr was a tenant farmer with some 3000 acres; like others he toured England and Ireland extensively offering advice on every subject from stock-breeding to farm cottages. The smaller short-woolled sheep which covered the Wolds and Heath when Defoe visited the county and the long-woolled variety in the Fens and Marsh were replaced by new breeds, the 'Improved Lincoln' bred from Bakewell's 'New Leicester' rams and 'Old Lincoln' ewes, and later the 'Lincolnshire Longwools', for many

86

years one of the most common breeds in England and abroad but now rare. New fodder crops meant that these animals could be pastured in large numbers on the heathlands: Cobbett saw 'innumerable flocks of those big, long-woolled sheep [in] thirty or forty acre fields with four or five or six hundred ewes, each with her own one or two lambs'. Other farm stock were developed: the Lincolnshire Curly Coat pig and the Wildmore 'Tits', a hardy fen pony, both had a high reputation, but the breeding of horses declined though horse fairs at Corby and especially Horncastle, the largest in the country, survived for some time.

Lincolnshire long-woolled sheep

Labour and machines

The changes in agriculture demanded more not less labour, so that although there was some migration to the towns from about 1821 most of the villages grew. Work seems to have become more seasonal, and women and children, often organised into gangs under a gangmaster, were pressed into service especially on the Heath and Cliff. Later considerable numbers of Irish labourers came in.

The Lincolnshire labourer in the 19th century was very mobile; he often served only one or two years before moving at the annual hiring fair to another farm perhaps no more than two or three miles away. This may, it is true, be a sign that the Lincolnshire farmworker was relatively well off, for many at the time held that compared with those in other counties, he was reasonably prosperous; when he was not needed on the land he could find work in the growing river trade, in fishing or catering for holiday-makers on the coast, in the newer quarrying or engineering industries or in occasional labour on the roads, canals and railways. But others commented on the extreme poverty of the village dweller in the early 19th century and pointed to the lack of new industries as in the Midlands and the north. The truth probably lies somewhere in the middle.

Certainly agriculture remained the region's principal employer up to 1851. Indeed the plentiful labour may even have held back the introduction of machinery on the farms: why spend money on machines when men and women can do the job? But another reason for the slow adoption of machinery was the opposition of the labourers. During an outbreak of violence and disorder the *Stamford Mercury* reported (1830):

> the panic among the Lincolnshire farmers is universal, particularly such as have threshing machines on their premises. Many have received threatening letters; and the breaking of machines, and conflagration of property, form the unvarying theme of conservation amongst all ranks of society.

One of these letters was sent to Joseph Stevens of Baumber near Horncastle in 1831:

> Steveson, you may think it a great favour that we write before we fire. If you have a machine in your yard, we will set fire to the stacks the first opportunity, and we can do it if you stand by; and you and all the farmers must give better wages to the labourers, or we will fire; and if fire will not do we will dredge poison on your turnip shells. You may warn all the farmers.

Farmers formed a Volunteer Corps and trained in earnest on the Heath. Harsh penalties were meted out to those caught: Priscilla Woodford, aged 15, a servant, was found guilty at Lincoln in 1832 of setting fire to a stack of hay, the property of Isaac Teesdale at Hacconby, and was transported for life.

But the campaign was over by the time machines came to be used extensively on Lincolnshire farms. The second agricultural revolution, fertilisers, new crops, steam engines, came late to the county; hand reaping with scythe English-style and sickle Irish-style was still common in the 1860s. From 1851 population fell in many villages and this has continued with some fluctuations ever since. Whether this fall is caused by or led to the use of machinery on the farms is not clear, but what was described in 1881 as 'the best farming which England can show' used less labour than before.

Road sign, Cowbit

88

XI Religion and the Community

'The prosperity of agriculture', wrote Arthur Young in 1799, 'as of everything else, depends on the moral and religious habits of the people'; and he recounted the perhaps apocryphal story of the Lincolnshire parish clerk who prevented service being said for five weeks because her pet goose was sitting in the pulpit. Such 'neglect of worship', it was alleged, was particularly prevalent in the Wolds.

A survey of church life in the county in 1788-92 supports Young's description. There was widespread non-residence among the clergy — three-quarters of Lincolnshire rectors and vicars served their parishes by visits or by curates. Some like Lord Bristol's agent Waterson at Sleaford accumulated benefices and lived in style on one of them, and evidence of neglect of pastoral functions abounds. One reason was that many livings were very poor, less than £50 p.a., and even the bishop admitted that dissenting teachers were often more learned than his own clergy.

Other forms of Christian observance emerged to meet spiritual and social needs in neglected parishes. At first they were closely interrelated: the three main groups of Anglicans, Catholics and Protestant dissenters had much in common, and transfer from one to another took place on occasion. The parents of John Wesley were both prominent dissenters before Samuel was ordained into the Church of England, while Wesley, himself an ordained Anglican, returned (voluntarily or involuntarily) to the nonconformist arena. This interrelationship did not break down until the 19th century; as late as the 1850s, the 'all but universal [practice] in this part of Lincolnshire at least [Swaby] the attendance of members both at church and chapel' was reported from town and village alike; at Lincoln 'they go from church to church, from chapel to church, and from church to chapel', while among the Methodist groups an 'acceptable preacher' was used by congregations of different persuasions without any sense of incongruity. All three strands were equally affected by the major movements of this period, evangelical enthusiasm and high church ritualism; prayer meetings, preachings and Bible study groups were features of all groups, just as increasing formalism and ornateness in buildings affected most denominations.

John and Charles Wesley

Religion and society

It has been argued that religion played its part in the destruction of traditional social structures. As distinct social classes emerged, the

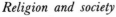

89

Frithville church

gentry in the 18th century, the middle classes of small owners and larger tenant farmers in the early 19th century, and the rural working classes not until the middle or late 19th century, the gentry identified more closely with the established church, the Anglican clergy drawn from the same families often joining them so that the church became increasingly remote from the people; the middle classes turned to the more 'polite' forms of dissent (Independents, Quakers, Unitarians and especially in Lincolnshire the Wesleyans), while the working classes retained at least for a time aspects of traditional communal patterns of life in the enthusiastic forms of worship associated with the Primitive Methodists and other groups.

Such an analysis needs more study before it can be accepted with confidence. So too does the relationship between urban and rural religion in the county. It seems that the towns gradually became the focal points for religion, subjecting rural centres of worship to an urban ethos. The government of the churches, their committees and courts, their major festivals and their leading figures tended more and more to be centred on the towns, so that to serve an urban congregation came to be regarded as a career advancement.

Such trends helped to undermine the cohesion of the local community. The solidarity of the village was not significantly threatened by the emergence of recusants, early dissenting groups and even the Wesleyans, but from the second quarter of the 19th century the 'gathered congregations' of the Primitive Methodists, Baptists and Independents led increasingly to new attitudes towards a hierarchically ordered local society. Lay participation in these groups (rare in the Church of England despite the parish officers of sexton, clerk and churchwarden) led to increased alienation from the established church and contributed to the disintegration of the community; it is not without significance that many chapels were built outside the villages, often on parish boundaries between local communities, a sign of this disintegration. The Church of England reacted, seeking to retain its primacy and identification with the community as a whole. It embarked on a rebuilding programme and in an attempt to win back those who now openly declared that they no longer belonged began to introduce more services: at Humberston in 1833 two services on Sunday were 'looked upon as opposition by the Methodists'; 'those Dissenters who were constantly attending Morning Service murmured and stayed from church because the Afternoon Service interfered with their chapel hour'. 'My evening duty has most woefully thinned their ranks', wrote the rector of Grimsby in 1829. Bishop Kaye urged his clergy to feed their flocks so that they no longer 'turned to any teacher who professes to supply them with spiritual food for which they hunger', and some responded: 'now at each service, a sermon is preached. It is hoped that the sermon in the morning will bring a larger congregation' (Hibaldstow, 1851). The Church of England in the villages became to a large extent just another denomination.

It is with such trends that the historian of religion in Lincolnshire will be concerned in the future rather than with the separate history of the denominations. Religion must as far as possible be seen as a whole, whether it is the various branches of the Christian church or the popular religion of magic, witchcraft, superstitions and customs. But until this work has been done, we must be content to describe the fortunes of the main forms of Christian activity in the county, and the late 18th-century survey which shows the distribution of these groupings at that time provides a useful starting point.

Catholics

Catholicism survived in Lincolnshire in small pockets, usually dependent upon a landholder who provided protection or even coercion. At Irnham where 77 per cent of the population were Catholic, 'Lord Arundell has a House here with a Chaplain where Mass is celebrated', and people from neighbouring Corby attended the Irnham chapel until it was removed to Corby early in the 19th century. Catholics were grouped in the upper Ancholme valley centred on the Heneage estate at Hainton (where a third of the population was 'papist'), in the north (Worlaby and an early church at Osgodby) and scattered over the central Wolds. Although there was a group of recusants in Lincoln at the end of the previous century, by 1790 this had apparently died out.

Roman Catholic church, Grantham

During the 19th century, Catholicism in the county was strengthened by a wave of immigrants, some from the continent, others from Ireland engaged in seasonal labour. Much of this New Catholicism with its priests who were not local men seems to have been despised by the older Catholic families for its irregularity in attending mass, its poverty and for listening to service while standing 'in the yard and outside the chapel door'. Only in Grantham did a long-established Catholic church supported by the Manners and Thorold families adapt itself to the new conditions of the 19th century.

Dissenters

The East Midlands were the centre of English 'separatism'; at least four Calvinist congregations in south Lincolnshire dated from the days of the Commonwealth, while Baptists were meeting in Epworth as early as 1623. The Axholme groups had declined by the 1790s. The General Baptists, strongly represented in the Fens between Boston and Long Sutton, were torn by the debate which turned most of them into Unitarians. David Taylor from Yorkshire established a New Connexion of Baptists at a conference in Lincoln in 1769, but it was driven out by the Old Connexion and only one chapel remained at Boston. Evangelicalism had relatively little impact on Old Dissent in Lincolnshire.

There was a sharp fall in the number of Presbyterian congregations; a few became Unitarian. They lay scattered over the county until in 1844 the Lincolnshire Association of Independent Ministers and Churches drew them closer together. The Quakers were strong in north

91

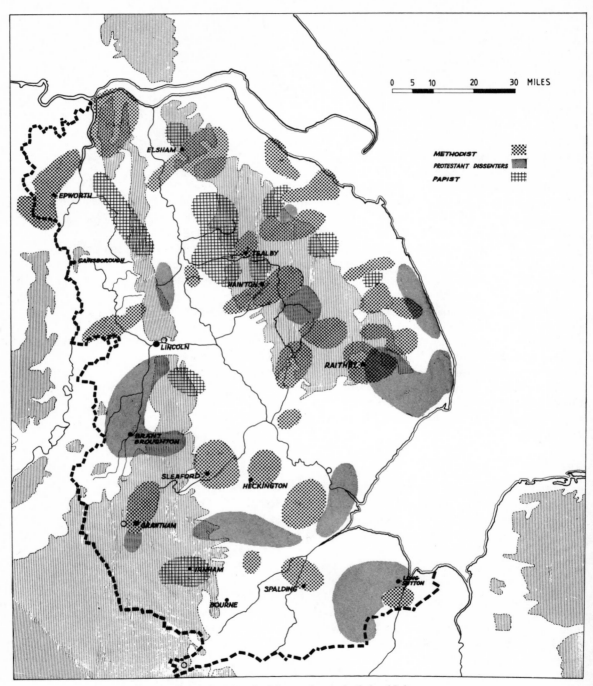

20. Religion in Lincolnshire at the end of the 18th century.

west Kesteven, the Marsh and the south and west Wolds. Like the Old Catholics they relied upon patronage to support them through the periods of intermittent and never very harsh persecution. But patronage could not protect them from decline, and the nearly 30 congregations of the early 18th century were reduced to nine by the mid-19th century; like the Independents their strength now lay in towns like Caistor, Lincoln and Spalding. Mormons appeared in the county before 1845, preaching in the public houses; despite mob violence as at Spalding, they established a number of congregations which grew slowly since 'the greater part of the members have emigrated' (1851).

The north of the county had a number of prominent Quaker families centred on the Society at Gainsborough but few other dissenters; it was in the Fens that these groups made their greatest impact – at Spalding, Gedney and Long Sutton with lesser centres at Bourne and elsewhere. Small congregations were often linked together for purposes of ministry: in 1720 'Joseph Hooke was ordained Pastor of the [Baptist] Church meeting in Bourne, Hackonby, Spalding and the Park adjacent'. Throughout the period there seems to have been little persecution although at Spalding the worshippers 'came out and fell to pulling apple trees and pair trees' when the constables called.

Methodists

Lincolnshire claims a special place in the history of the Evangelical Revival as the home of John and Charles Wesley. Their father held the livings of South Ormesby and later for 39 years of Epworth and Wroote in Axholme. Here John and Charles with their brother Samuel and their many sisters were educated by their father and mother before being sent to Oxford where they established their rigorous society, seeking salvation by discipline. They went to Georgia to serve the colonists there, seeking salvation in mission; but it was in London that first Charles and later John were converted under the influence of the Moravian Christian Brethren. Then followed a life of preaching, debating, organising societies and settling disputes throughout the country.

Epworth Rectory

Wesley's first three centres were at London, Bristol and Newcastle upon Tyne. Lincolnshire came later. His was a mission to the nation, particularly the towns in which increasingly large populations lived in poverty, ignorance, hard labour and crime. Wesley was a figure of the new age, not the old one which Lincolnshire represented in the 18th century. But both Wesleys and their supporters were active in the county, especially in the north; on at least one occasion John faced a riotous mob at Crowle. Congregations were established early and Methodism became stronger in this county than in most other parts of the country. There were large numbers in the Sleaford area (half the population of Heckington in 1790), in the south Wolds (Raithby, 62 per cent) and in the north Wolds.

As with the Catholics, sometimes the aristocracy took the lead like the Tennysons at Tealby, though at Elsham John Wesley found the landowners hostile and at Appleby the Winns (squire and parson) drove the Wesleyans out. But in general the movement seems to have been based on the newer class of freehold or substantial tenant farmer like the Ellis family of Burton on Stather or George Milns in the Marsh.

The 1851 census of religion shows the increase in the number of Methodist meeting houses between 1790 and 1850. Before their chapels were built, congregations met in cottages, barns and outhouses. The 'agitations' which split the movement in 1797, 1835 and 1849 and local schisms created more congregations so that in some villages there were two or three Methodist groups each with its own chapel. The sect flourished in open villages like Binbrook and Tetford in the north or Brant Broughton (which housed Quaker and two Methodist chapels) and Corby in the south; growing towns like Brigg became 'a haven for dissenters and a seminary for all such like cattle the whole county over'.

Anglicans

Not all religious enthusiasm and discipline lay with the nonconformists any more than all neglect and corruption lay with the established church. There were it is true drunken and immoral Anglican clergy as at Coningsby in the early 18th century, but equally the Baptist minister at Bourne in 1794 'turned out a very bad man. He was under necessity to leave the town in the night for fear of the mob; drunkenness and sodomy were laid to his charge'. And there were many 'Godly and pious Pastors' in Lincolnshire parishes. The extensive use of curates did not necessarily lead to neglect for they often lived in the same parish for many years, serving under successive rectors or vicars, and thus became identified with their parishioners.

Nor were the buildings always neglected. Some new churches were built like Stainfield (1711), Harmston (1717), Wilsthorpe near Greatford (1715) and Langton by Spilsby (1725), and older churches were restored, often at great cost. With the growing population and the new settlements established after enclosure, drainage and waste reclamation, new parishes were created and new churches and chapels endowed. The Fens, where the Church was at its weakest, witnessed the building or rebuilding (often in brick) of churches as at Sutton St Edmund and West Pinchbeck. The new villages of East, West and Wildmore Fen were dowered by Act of Parliament (1812) with churches, but in places temporary premises were needed as at New Holland where first the railway station waiting room and later the schoolroom were used for worship until the church was completed. In the expanding towns, new parish churches were erected and endowed. Bishop, lay patron, incumbents, Church societies and trusts, local lay subscribers, drainage commissioners – all sources of revenue were pressed into service to outstrip the dissenters and put up new and better buildings or restore older often crumbling centres of local religious life.

Three main movements affected the Church of England in Lincolnshire between 1750 and 1850. First it felt the winds of the Evangelical

Revival. Clergy like John Pugh of Rauceby friend of Charles Simeon and founder of the Church Missionary Society and John Wilson of Donington led the way in bringing new ideas and a new spirit into the worship of the day. Some like Charles Dodsworth of Welby even helped build Wesleyan chapels in their parishes.

Swaton Vicarage

Secondly the bishops of Lincoln launched a programme of reform particularly directed against the non-residence and pluralism of many of their clergy. The 'vicarage movement' of the 1830s and 1840s, aimed at supplying a decent parsonage house in every parish, thus eliminating one excuse for non-residence, has given us many of the surviving Lincolnshire vicarages, substantial houses in brick or stone. But perhaps more effective in reducing pluralism was the increase in the value of rural benefices at this time; Bishop Kaye tried to ensure that every incumbent had at least £200 p.a.

The work of these reforming bishops – John Kaye, Christopher Wordsworth and Edward King – eventually bore fruit. The 'squarson' like the Beriges of Algarkirk and Fosdyke and the Winns at Appleby became rarer; even John King who lived at Ashby de la Launde Hall and owned, bred and trained racehorses and who described clergymen like himself as 'only a particular variety of country gentlemen' was called to account.

Kaye urged the increase of Sunday services and preaching but his encouragement of a weekly communion took longer to bear fruit; Lincolnshire was well behind other areas in this respect in the 1840s and 1850s. Bishop King turned his attention to the towns like Grimsby. All the bishops and many of the clergy emphasised the importance of education as an antidote to the 'manner in which the people have been neglected. A great number of people attend no place of worship. There is a wide field for exertion but as is universally the case, no great good can be done without an established school'.

Thirdly came the High Church movement – the twin threads of ritualism and Anglo-Catholic doctrine promoted locally by the Ecclesiological Societies in Louth and elsewhere. It was largely from this that the demand for the restoration of so many parish churches originated. High church practices spread rapidly despite opposition; Thomas Pelham-Dale, rector of Sausthorpe, went to prison for his 'excessive religious zeal', and even Bishop King fought a High Court suit over the use of cope and mitre. In the 1860s, Thomas Wimberley Mossman of Torrington trained his 'Mossman Monks' to go preaching in Lincoln and Louth and eventually resigned his living to join the Catholic church.

But the majority of clergy were more interested in those whom 'distance and want of decent apparel' kept from attending church rather than with dogma. They were concerned for the local community as a whole. 'I endeavour to avoid all irritation', wrote the rector of Swaby in relation to his Wesleyan neighbours, 'and so we jog on together, as friendly as possible'. They were anxious to defuse the tithe and church rate war which racked many villages at this time. Perhaps they were aware that the 'revived practices' separated the priest further from his people and led to deteriorating relations with Methodists and others. Rivalry between church and chapel certainly grew and extended to the schools; the race between the Anglicans and the free churches to establish a school in every village had begun. The hostility has left its mark on some Lincolnshire villages today. In Corby it is said that relations between the Anglicans and the Catholics in the late 19th century were closer than those between the Anglicans and the Methodists, and apart from the Anglican Grammar school, there were three rival elementary schools, Catholic, Methodist and Board school (of which the Anglican incumbent was chairman).

Wilsthorpe church

35. Joseph Ruston (1835–97), the pioneer of Lincoln's engineering.

36. Employees of the Appleby Iron Company, June 1887: note the pig-iron in the railway wagon.

37. One of Grimsby's horse-drawn trams (1890).

38. Saddle tank *Bismarck* in the newly-opened Alexandra Dock, Grimsby (1879).

39. The first 'Steam Navvy', made by Ruston's of Lincoln.

40. Five-sail tower mill near Alford, built for grinding cereals for fodder.

41. Lode Bank steam pump drainage station on Hobhole Drain near Stickney.

42. The Trent riverside at Gainsborough, showing flour mills and warehousing from the great days of river traffic

XII Roads, Rivers and Railways

The changes which Lincolnshire saw in the 18th and 19th century were closely linked to improved means of communication. As the land produced more, markets were sought further afield in the industrial Midlands and north; new techniques called for materials such as fertilisers not always available locally, and the spread of innovative ideas was related to traffic routes. Improved roads and waterways, and later the new railways were created by and contributed to the agricultural revolution.

Roads

Lincolnshire's roads were bad; the broad-wheeled wagon and the droves of cattle passing over long distances helped to make it almost impossible for parishes to keep even the main roads in their parish in good repair. They may not have been as bad as in some other parts of the country: the *Gentleman's Magazine* in 1774 thought the good roads reflected the wealth of the area, and Arthur Young, usually outspoken in his criticisms, was moderate:

> [the fen roads] generally made with silt or old sea sand . . . when moderately
> wet are very good; but dreadfully dusty and heavy in dry weather; . . . on
> a thaw they are like mortar . . . Take the county in general and they must
> be esteemed below par. (1799)

Turnpike milestone

Turnpike trusts sprang up to deal with this problem. Set up by Act of Parliament, they improved existing stretches or built new roads, charging tolls at the 'bars' set at intervals along the route. By the middle of the 18th century, the movement was in full flood, no less than 450 Acts being passed between 1760 and 1764, and the number of improved roads grew rapidly.

The way towards turnpikes in Lincolnshire was pointed in 1666 when the Deeping Fen commissioners secured rights over the roads in their drainage area similar to those enjoyed by the later turnpike trustees. The main series of Lincolnshire Acts came between 1755 and 1765 when an average of one trust each year was set up covering more than 180 miles of road. By 1834, 29 trusts had been set up controlling between 450 and 500 miles of road in the county. Eight trusts were large with more than 20 miles each; 18 trusts had between ten and 20 miles, and three were small, with less than ten miles of road under their care. In all, Lincolnshire had 15 per cent of its roads turnpiked, rather more than other large counties like Essex, Suffolk and especially Norfolk but

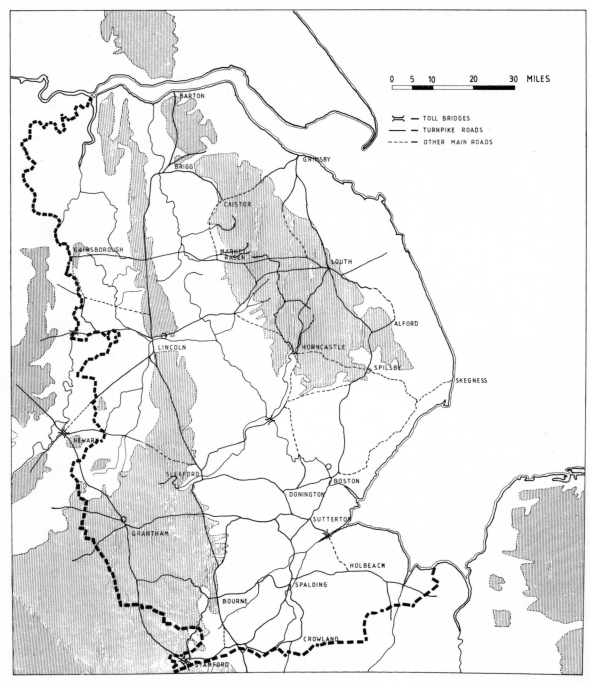

21. The Main Roads.

much less than smaller ones like Huntingdonshire, Derbyshire and Staffordshire.

The trusts built toll houses, laid out branch roads and on occasion cut off side roads; they took over some of the streets in the towns they passed through: most of the main roads through Lincoln were turnpiked between 1755 and 1797. By 1765 they had laid out the outlines of the present trunk road system of the county. From that date, most new schemes were associated with drainage such as the Boston-Bourne road (1765) and the East Fen reclamation (1801-7), but new routes were thrust through the Fens towards King's Lynn like the Swineshead-Fosdyke road (1826) and the bridge and causeway over the Nene at Sutton Bridge (1831).

Turnpike toll house, Anwick

This last road soon grew to be the most important highway in the Fens. The two other major through routes in the county were the Great North Road, turnpiked between Grantham and Newark in 1725-6 (the earliest Act for the county) and between Grantham and Stamford in 1738-9, and secondly the route from London to the Humber. The first part of this road, from Peterborough to Lincoln, was turnpiked in 1755; it entered the county at Market Deeping where the London-Lincoln coaches (posting at the Bull Inn) met the Boston-Leicester coaches (the New Inn) and passed via Bourne and Sleaford to Lincoln; the Lincoln-Barton ferry road was turnpiked in 1765. The Lincoln-Peterborough was the most powerful trust in the county. Divided into six districts, it controlled a number of branch routes; roads ran from Bourne, for instance, westwards to the Great North Road at Colsterworth, eastwards into the Fens at Spalding and northwards to Donington and Boston. It abandoned the prehistoric Mareham Lane south of Sleaford in favour of the road through Folkingham, and early in the 19th century created a new road from Sleaford to Lincoln across open wasteland so bare that Sir Francis Dashwood had built a 'land lighthouse' at Dunston to guide travellers. The Act for this route was the most costly turnpike Act of all.

Three main roads crossed the county from west to east. The Bawtry-Hainton road (1765) crossed the Trent and opened access into Yorkshire, and the Newark-Sleaford road (1759) and the Grantham-Donington road (1804) gave Boston its overland routes.

Traffic, both goods and passengers, increased. By the 1830s four stage coach routes ran from London to Lincolnshire destinations and five passed through the county on their way north; another three ran from west to east and 21 local routes from town to town. The four day journey from Barton to London was cut to 36 hours by 1786, and further improvements followed the introduction of the mail coach on local (Lincoln-Boston 1804) and national (London-Boston 1807) routes. The Boston mail was extended to Louth in 1818 and in 1827 'the Postmaster General is making arrangements for continuing the London Mail from Louth to Grimsby, which will make the journey from London to Grimsby possible in 27 hours [connecting with] the two daily packet boats to

Bourne town hall

Hull' (*Stamford Mercury*). By the 1830s seven Royal Mail coaches were passing into or through Lincolnshire every day: 'until a few years ago, no coaches passed through Gainsborough; now [1817] there is one . . . every day to Doncaster, Wakefield, Leeds, and another to Manchester. Also one to Lincoln three days a week, and returns next day in time for passengers to go by steam packet to Hull, or forward to Doncaster, etc.'.

The turnpikes encouraged the J.P.s in their quarter sessions and the parish officers to improve their 'terrible bad roads'. They copied the methods used by the trust engineers like McAdam (employed on the Grantham-Nottingham and Leadenham-Mansfield roads, 1826); indeed the Brigg magistrates ordered the turnpike trustees to engage a surveyor who could advise on McAdam's principles of road building. Local residents could begin to rejoice in 'such a change as seldom experienced when but a few years ago the roads hereabouts were hardly passable'.

But despite the fact that they could call on 'statute labour' and on occasion paupers from the parishes to help with those stretches of road which ran through the parish, the trusts could not always keep up their roads. Arthur Young reported:

> From Grimsthorpe to Colsterworth are eight miles, called by courtesy of the neighourhood, a Turnpike; but in which we were in every moment either buried in quagmires of mud or racked to dislocation over pieces of rock which they term mending. A great house must be great indeed to answer the fatigue, pain and anxiety of such approaches. No environs are so truly magnificent as good roads in a country which abounds in bad. Pity that the tolls are not trebled.

The cause was largely financial. Large initial sums were needed for the Act and the building of roads and bridges: the road between Brigg and Lincoln (1765) cost some £80-120 per mile, the Fosdyke bridge (1812-15) cost £20,000. Part of these sums were raised from investors, large and small. Sir Joseph Banks was an example of the larger investor; he put money into the Sleaford-Tattershall and Grimsby trusts as well as into two navigation schemes and at least one bridge-building company. At the other end of the scale, the parish officers of Gedney invested small sums left for charitable purposes in the King's Lynn-Holbeach trust. But the rest of the capital came from mortgaging the tolls; thus for many years the income due to the trustees from the toll bars passed into other hands. Dividends went to meet loan charges and other costs; the Sleaford-Tattershall trust paid no dividend for the first 30 years and only paid in 1825 because of 'the said Road having ever since the 25th day of June 1816 been supported and kept in repair by and at the expence of the several Parishes thro' which it extends'. The trusts pressed all sources of support into service. Some collected part of the parish highway rates, and sometimes even parish charities were diverted to this purpose (Gainsborough and Louth). The struggle to maintain these roads was great, especially since in many cases there was a good deal of opposition from local landowners who on occasion diverted the proposed road away from their estates (the duke of Ancaster agreed to maintain the extra third of a mile needed to make the new road go round rather than

*Brigg
town hall*

100

through Grimsthorpe Park), from those who had interests affected by the roads, and from some local residents who, resentful at new barriers across their traditional routes, repeatedly broke the bars and side gates (as at South Elkington) and refused to pay the tolls even when these were discounted for them.

Greyhound
Inn,
Folkingham

But by the 1820s the situation had improved. Floods and other hazards still interrupted traffic: as late as the 1850s the roads at Gedney 'are almost impassable' in winter, while in 1804 the 'London to Barton-on-Humber mail on Sunday night was attacked by three footpads at the bottom of Elsham Hill' (*Hull Advertiser*). But the greatly increased traffic after the end of the Napoleonic wars boosted the profits. In 1780 the Lincoln-Boston tolls were estimated at £300 p.a.; in 1810 they were offered at lease at £3000 p.a. And the roads improved: whereas in 1821 some 72 per cent of the county's turnpike roads were said to be in a bad way, parliament was told in 1840 that, of the 29 Lincolnshire trusts, 21 were efficient and only two were responsible for bad roads.

The difference between the turnpikes and the parish roads was striking: the main roads were 'good at all seasons. The bye-roads . . . are on the contrary very bad for at least six months in the year'. These 'cursed roads' (Tetney, 1800) received some attention: 'in one year we [the parish of Winterton] have expended nearly seven hundred pounds on the roads', while at Burgh le Marsh 'the inhabitants of this district . . . at immense expense . . . have procured materials from a considerable distance and have put their principal roads into excellent repair, without calling in the aid of a Turnpike Act'. But nearly five times as much was spent on each mile of turnpike road as on the non-turnpiked parish roads: in 1836, £40,000 was spent by the trusts on 450 miles of turnpikes, while in 1839 a total of £80,664 was incurred by all the parish officers on some 4620 miles of roads.

The turnpikes changed the face of the county. Few parts of the region found themselves out of reach of at least one passable road. Villages, especially in the Fens, became less isolated and regional differences declined as travel became easier. New river crossings, like the Trent bridge at Gainsborough (1787), the Witham bridge at Tattershall (1795, the first on the river between Lincoln and Boston) and the bridges over the Welland at Fosdyke and over the Nene at Sutton Bridge opened up whole new possibilities.

Waterways

Rivers formed an important part of Lincolnshire's transport system from early times. The prehistoric dug-outs, the Roman canals, the carriage of Ancaster stone to Nottingham and Louth for medieval building works all testify to the use of the waterways. Land routes remained valuable – the food needed for the Lincoln parliament in 1301 came overland from Grimsby, Stamford and Barton, not by water; but both people and goods moved by water through the region. The new rector of Coningsby in 1730 rode from London to Donington and then

101

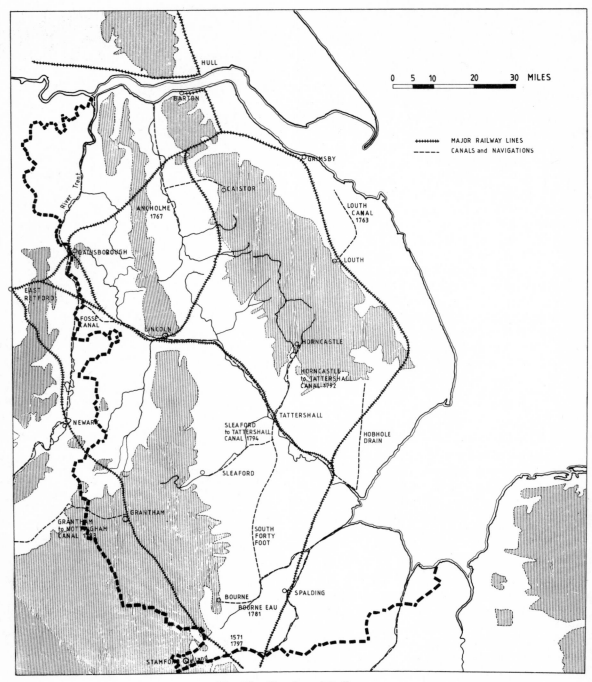

22. The Canals and Railways.

went by boat, being 'met on the water' by the curate and churchwardens; and a 17th-century coal merchant on the Trent wrote that 'the convenien-cye for carriadg by water is muche to further the sale att an easier rate to manie markett towns'.

Lincolnshire looked more to the sea and the coastal trade with London than to connections with the Midlands. Apart from the Fosse Dyke between the Witham at Lincoln and the Trent, only one route westwards was successful, the Grantham-Nottingham canal; other plans to link the county with the Midlands were abortive. Most of the county's schemes were navigations rather than canals; the aim was to make the rivers, which were liable to silt up as a result of frequent flooding, navigable rather than to link town with town. The first drainage and embanking schemes channelled the flow of water and for a time improved the scour, but drainage led to the peat shrinking and further flooding occurred. One of the earliest schemes was the Act relating to the Welland at Stamford (1570) but despite strenuous efforts throughout the 17th century this navigation never flourished. An attempt (1671) to canalise the Witham between Boston and Lincoln was equally ineffective.

The Ellison family, father and son, who improved the Fosse Dyke in the 1740s and made large profits, showed the way to success, and between 1760 and 1830 some 20 Acts were passed covering 10 schemes in the county. The work fell into clearly marked phases.In the 1760s, the Witham and Ancholme were improved and a canal built from Louth to Tetney on the coast. Then came a lull: a half-hearted attempt to link Bourne with the Glen and Welland by Bourne Eau and (inspired by the extensive works in Nottinghamshire next door which pushed the limits of navigation on the Trent up river beyond Nottingham to Long Eaton) a number of unsuccessful plans – to join Alford to the sea, Grantham with Newark or Stamford with the Midlands – were all that materialised. A third stage started in 1791 and five schemes were completed in a short time – the Slea Navigation (1791-4), the Nottingham-Grantham canal (the biggest scheme at its date, 1793-8), the Caistor canal (1793), the Keadby canal across Axholme to the Trent (1793, 'really a Yorkshire canal which strayed into Lincolnshire') and the Horncastle Navigation (planned in 1787 but not opened until 1802). The first 10 years of the 19th century saw the last stage, with improvements to the Ancholme (1802) and Witham (1808) and the building of navigable drains like Hobhole and the South Forty Foot (1806-8) in the course of draining the Fens. More abortive proposals were made, in the Marsh, the Ancholme valley, the region around Stamford and most ambitious of all a link canal between Grantham and Sleaford.

Schemes often took a long time to complete; the Louth-Tetney project despite the support of the town corporation took 14 years. Opposition feared drainage disasters and damage to local interests, and on occasion local notables were mobilised like lord Bertie for the Witham Act (1762). Drainage engineers like Grundy of Spalding and Jessop of Newark built them; John Rennie was engaged on the Grimsby Docks

Seal of
Grimsby Haven
Company

when called to drain the Fens and cut the navigable drains around Boston.

By 1800 the main market towns of the county like Horncastle had direct access by water to the sea, and the drainage channels provided navigable waterways to large numbers of smaller market centres and villages. Both people and goods passed along these routes. From the Witham Navigation Act 1812, for instance, packet boats passed down the river every Wednesday and Saturday, calling at isolated public houses (*Anchor Inn*, etc), picking up parcels and passengers for Boston market. From all over the Fens they poured into the town via the drains and their outlets, Bargate Bridge, Grand Sluice and Black Sluice, and Boston grew into a major corn market, sending potatoes to London and importing fertilisers, coal and timber. Market boats operated along the Ancholme into Brigg. Prosperity came to some of the river-bank dwellers. Gainsborough took over from West Stockwith as the centre for Trent traffic (an earlier attempt had been made to found a port at Susworth), and new port facilities were provided at inland towns like Louth (Riverhead). Early factories and warehouses grew up alongside the wharves as at Grantham and Lincoln (Brayford Pool). The unsuccessful industrial village of New Bolingbroke was to have relied heavily on water transport.

Steam packet boat

But waterways, like the turnpikes, were costly to build and to maintain. The new cut at Grimsby cost £20,000, and £21,000 was spent on the unfinished Horncastle-Witham Navigation; the trustees in both cases were alleged to 'have managed so as to waste such money ... many thousand pounds were very ill spent'. New Acts were required to raise extra capital. At Horncastle, one of the most difficult waterways in the county to build, it took 20 years to pay off the debts. Even the rich Sleaford-Witham Navigation paid no dividend from the start in 1794 until 1811. But eventually the investment paid off; by 1824 the tolls on the Sleaford Navigation had risen from £500 to more than £1000 p.a., and on the Grantham canal (which had cost some £100,000 for 33 miles of waterway) the tolls at the end of the 18th century were almost £5000 p.a. As with the turnpikes, these tolls were often mortgaged or leased on long and favourable terms to local entrepreneurs like Charles Chaplin at Louth. The same people were involved: Benjamin Handley called a meeting in 1792 to discuss the Sleaford-Witham Navigation; also present were Anthony Peacock and Edward Waterson, both engaged in the Sleaford enclosure and local turnpike schemes.

Railways

Railways came late to Lincolnshire; it was almost the last county to be touched. The first two lines (Nottingham-Lincoln and Stamford-Peterborough) were opened in 1846, 16 years after the Liverpool-Manchester railway had proved such schemes profitable.

One reason for the delay was the relatively small demand for the carriage of bulk cargoes. Lincolnshire's livestock was moved on the hoof,

104

its grain by water. But above all there was indecision about which routes to follow. As early as the 1820s plans were drawn up for lines through the county to York (John Rennie, 1827 and the G.N.R., 1833) or to link inland towns to the coast (even Liverpool-Grimsby, 1831). The major problem was the route north. The crossing of the Fens was not easy and the limestone belt involved tunnelling; the line had either to proceed on the east side of the limestone linking Peterborough, Sleaford, Lincoln and Gainsborough (the 'Fens' route) or cross the higher land linking Stamford, Grantham and Gainsborough (the 'Towns' route which it was generally agreed would cost more but carry more traffic). The battle was long and hard, especially in 1844-5 but in the end parliament settled on a modified Towns route (Peterborough, Grantham, Newark and Retford). Passions ran high: bells were rung in Stamford, a civic meeting in Lincoln broke up in disorder and it is claimed that 8000 people from all over the county crowded into Lincoln castle to hear the routes debated. Meanwhile the railways were getting steadily nearer, Nottingham (1839), Leicester and Hull (1840), and the people of Lincolnshire used the coaches promoted by the railway companies to the nearer stations, particularly Rotherham and Leicester; Louth was joined by coach to Peterborough when the railway arrived there (1845).

When building began (1845-6), the first lines came in a rush; a third of the county's railways, 220 miles, were opened before 1850. There were four main routes. In 1848-9 the Manchester, Sheffield and Lincolnshire Company, at the insistence of the new Grimsby Dock Company and Sheffield industrialists, drove a line through the north of the county linking Grimsby with south Yorkshire. Secondly, the East Lincolnshire Railway Company opened the Grimsby-Boston line through Alford and Louth; it was extended to the New Holland ferries which the railway companies and local interests were developing. Thirdly, the G.N.R. completed its 'Loop' line from Peterborough through Boston to Lincoln to join the London-York line at Bawtry (1847-9).

The Loop line was opened before the Towns line across the Kesteven uplands was completed. The G.N.R. was in difficulties. The L.N.E.R. had already built its London-Edinburgh route, but the G.N.R. only had the stretches south of Lincolnshire and north of the county finished; the company was held up on the middle section for 'about 15 miles in the immediate neighbourhood of Grantham . . . on which occur rather heavy works, requiring a longer time to complete that the rest of the Towns Line', as the chairman reported in 1849. The route passed up the Glen valley and crossed to the Witham valley through the Stoke tunnel. The cost was high, some £25,000 per mile compared with an average of £13,000 for the rest of the line, and the work was not finished until 1852. The directors thus decided to build the Loop line 'which could be made in 18 months [so that] the Company was getting the traffic, such as it was, from that in the meantime'.

By 1852 the main arteries in the county had been laid down. Lincolnshire's place in the national network is seen from the fact that only one town, Grantham, had direct links with both London and the north. Two other main lines were built, the Ambergate-Boston line (1857-9) and a route from Lincoln across the Fens to Spalding and on to March and East Anglia (1867-82). The rest was infilling, short lines between towns; the longest new lines in Lincolnshire after 1852 were Sutton Bridge-Peterborough (26 miles, 1866) and Spalding-Ruskington (21 miles, 1882).

Early steam engine

The county was divided over the railways. Henry Handley of Culverthorpe M.P. supported the Towns line while his political rivals Charles Chaplin of Blankney and Lord Worsley, the earl of Yarborough's son, urged the Fens line. Landowners and businessmen raised capital, launched small companies and built lines, leasing them to the great companies; while others like Colonel Charles Sibthorpe of Lincoln, M.P. opposed the lines, refusing them access to land near their estates.

The railways brought long-term and short-term effects. Immediately there was the purchase of supplies. The Grimsthorpe estate agent 'had one of the Contractors for making the Railway at Little Bytham yesterday who came to see if we could supply him with sleepers'. The local farmer, retailer and craftsman made their profit: 'I have told Pilkington that he is allowed to brew small beer for the year only, and none of the beer to be drunk upon the premises'. In 1851, 600 railway workers were staying in six south Lincolnshire villages for work on the Towns line; all but two of the 313 workers in Castle and Little Bytham were immigrants. They lived in lodgings, huts, tents and barns, and they moved on when the work was done.

Long-term, places like Barnetby (a railway junction) benefited. Scunthorpe sent iron ore from 1860 to the Trent barges and from 1866, when Gunness railway bridge was opened in the face of opposition from Gainsborough merchants, direct to Sheffield. Docks at Grimsby accompanied the railway. Some places like Folkingham and Stamford attributed their slow growth to the lack of a railway. Life in the countryside became richer. Coal from Doncaster was readily available; the Ancaster estate agent (1855) 'sold about 60 tons and carried 31 tons to the Gardens, Stables, and Laundry at Grimsthorpe. We can get away from Bytham [station] in a day about 30 tons'. The cost of transporting stock, especially sheep, was high but fairs with a railway connection like Corby flourished. Fertilisers were brought in, grain sent out: 'I have this afternoon sent 5 stones wheaten flour to the Little Bytham station, which will be forwarded per Goods Train via Edinburgh to Glasgow Station'.

Although some of the turnpikes reported increased traffic, and tolls at bars closest to the stations, as on the Bourne-Colsterworth and Lincoln-Retford roads, rose, in general long distance road carriage declined. As early as 1841 before the railways had entered the county, the *Lincoln Gazette* printed an obituary:

> Died, on Friday last, the London and Leeds
> Mail-Coach in the fifth year of its age.
> The immediate cause of its dissolution is
> *the spread of Railways*'.

106

But local carriers became more important. Some canals were leased to the railway companies – the Fosse Dyke and the Grantham-Nottingham canal, and goods traffic continued (it even increased on the Fosse Dyke in the 1880s) until the 1920s and 1930s.But in the end the combined effects of the railways and the revived road traffic reduced the income from tolls so severely that the independent canal companies could no longer survive.

The railways also took a major share of passenger traffic. The Grantham-Lincoln line was opened on 15 April 1867 with a daily service of three stopping and two through trains each way. Coaches were timed to meet trains and at New Holland the trains and ferries met. Steam packets continued between Hull and Gainsborough, down the coast and up the Witham, but passenger traffic on these routes fell. From 1863 the Witham packet took goods rather than passengers into Boston, though passengers used the drains and the Ancholme longer – until in fact the rural bus provided a faster, more reliable and more flexible mode of transport.

The railways built the seaside resorts. At first the lines ignored the coast, and when they were extended it was to carry fertilisers and agricultural produce. In 1873 the first line to Skegness was built, extended to Mablethorpe in 1877, but trade rather than leisure predominated. Acts of parliament were secured for the establishment of docks on the coast at various points between Wainfleet and Sutton in the Marsh, to be linked by railway through Lincoln to the Midlands (the Lincoln-Chesterfield line of 1897 was part of these proposals), and a narrow gauge tramway ran between Alford and Sutton from 1884 and 1889. But the docks were never built and the proposals died when the Immingham docks were begun in 1906. Instead the holiday industry took over. In 1886 the first line specifically for the holiday-maker was built between Willoughby and Sutton, and Skegness was developed with the aid of the railway company. And the result of the railway development on the coast of Lincolnshire can be seen today; despite the fact that the holiday-maker now comes by car or bus and not by train, Skegness and its neighbouring resorts draw more on Midland towns like Nottingham, while Cleethorpes is still regarded as the resort for south Yorkshire.

The 'Jolly Fisherman'

XIII The Making of Modern Lincolnshire

The rate of population growth in 19th-century Lincolnshire was slower than elsewhere, and it fell off sharply after 1851. At first both towns and rural areas shared in the growth but most of the gains in the later years were focussed in a few towns and on the coast. The urban population of the county rose from 28 per cent in 1801 to 33 per cent in 1851 and to 46 per cent in 1901, but the towns were still small – in 1831 only six places had more than 5000 inhabitants.

As the towns grew, there was a decline in regional variations brought about by improved communications, better marketing of goods, and changes in farming and in the social structure of rural society. The drainage schemes and enclosure, followed by a depression in the 1820s, prosperity in the 1850s and a severe depression in the 1870s, encouraged the Lincolnshire farmer everywhere to diversify rather than to specialise. Throughout the county pasture gave way to arable, stock-rearing to corn or mixed farming. Lincolnshire became a major corn-producing area for the nation (wheat rather than barley) but it still had a substantial investment in sheep (28 per cent of the cultivated land was permanent pasture late in the century). The ring-fence farm became the focus of agricultural life rather than the estate or the local community. The farmer, both the freeholder and the tenant (protected as he was by the 'Lincolnshire Custom') and his family were the risk-takers, and the beneficiaries when times were good, rather than the landlord or the village as a whole. By 1900 there was more difference between town and country than between the Marsh and Heath, Fens and Wolds.

But regional variations did not disappear altogether. The Fens, which looked to Cambridgeshire and Norfolk, were the home of smallholders; they suffered less from the dislocation of enclosure and the depression of the 1820s and 1830s. The few gentry in this region contributed relatively little to the social and cultural life of the area, or of the county. Here, as elsewhere, grazing gave way to arable but from the 1860s the prosperity of the area declined and the emigration of younger sons became more common.

Lindsey and Kesteven were the home of the great landlords. In Lindsey the Pelham earls of Yarborough dominated from the Brocklesby estate. Lords Scarbrough and Willoughby d'Eresby who held extensive but scattered estates were non-resident, and the local gentry like Chaplin of Tathwell and Dixon of Holton le Moor emulated or opposed Yarborough. Like Nottinghamshire and south Yorkshire, large farms and

Street pump,
Caistor

wealthy farmers characterised the area, and sheep gave way to wheat. In Kesteven, which looked more towards Leicestershire and North-amptonshire, the influence of the Ancaster estate at Grimsthorpe was rivalled by the Brownlows of Belton and the Manners at Belvoir. A larger number of gentry, often of ancient Lincolnshire lines, resided on their lands – the Chaplins of Blankney, Thorolds, Welbys, Turnors, Whichcotes and others. They were conservative – and although the area saw an increase in corn (especially barley), sheep and cattle continued here longer than elsewhere in the county.

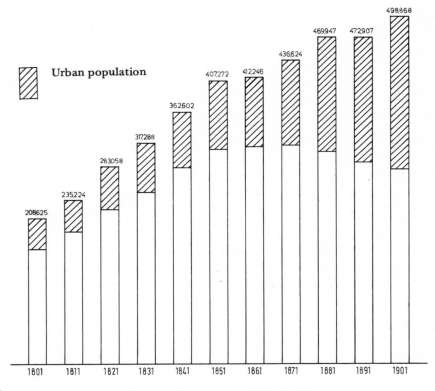

23. Rural and urban population in 19th-century Lincolnshire.

The differences and changes reflected themselves in the area's political history. In 1832 the number of county M.P.s was increased from two to four, but the number of town seats was reduced, until from 1867 county and town representation was merged into a few large rural constituencies. In the new constituency of North Lincolnshire, the earl of Yarborough's whig supporters, many of them tenants, outvoted the tory gentry of Lindsey, but in Kesteven the tory gentry outvoted the whig Ancaster supporters (though the Ancaster family eventually switched to the tories), in contrast to the parochialism, indecision and relative apathy of the voters of Holland.

The Marsh and Axholme were characterised by smaller farms, somewhat less prosperity and less innovativeness. And the coastal economy changed from fishing and wrecking (the Saltfleet wrecker waiting for his 'Godsend' was notorious: 'These Christian savages when they see a vessel driving on the beach, clap their hands and shout exaltingly, Thank God a Wreck'); the Lincolnshire Coast Association (1826) put a lifeboat at Gibraltar Point near Skegness, and inns for sea bathers sprang up at Cleethorpes, Saltfleet, Mablethorpe, Sutton, Skegness, Frieston and Fosdyke. Fuller development began in the 1840s, first at Cleethorpes, then at Mablethorpe-Sutton and Skegness.

Social changes

The emergence of class differences affected 19th-century Lincolnshire as elsewhere. The greater landlord, gentry, small owner and larger tenant farmer, smallholder, and labourer began to take their terms of reference from other members of the same class rather than from the community in which they resided. The distinctions were never entirely clear. The gentry and major landlords built similar houses (Harlaxton by Gregory, Stoke Rochford by Turnor, Denton by Welby, Revesby by Stanhope) and shared common interests like the Belvoir and Brocklesby Hunts. The gentry and the larger tenant farmers were both concerned about church and poor rates, tithes, corn prices and protectionism (particularly in Lindsey), malt taxes (especially on the Kesteven heathlands) and poaching (the Lincolnshire poacher was celebrated in song, and trainloads of poachers from Yorkshire were alleged to raid the region of Woodhall Spa). Many tenant farmers had held their farms for generations, investing large sums in the land and buildings, and came to regard the tenancy as family property to be handed down in the same way as freeholds.

Revesby Hall, home of the Banks family

The gentry and larger farmers joined together in Agricultural Societies which organised competitions, ploughing matches, stock shows, lectures, visits and publications, and spread ideas like Lord Yarborough's tree planting at Brocklesby or Henry Handley's use of steam in Kesteven. A county society existed from 1819 to the 1840s, mainly in Lindsey, with local ones in Caistor, Alford and Sutton. The North Lincolnshire Society, established in 1836, was extended to Kesteven and Holland in 1868.

The major social divide came between the farmer (gentleman or tenant) on the one hand and the smallholder and labourer on the other. The latter were more concerned with prices and inflation, unionism and the tied cottage. And this group formed the bulk of the county's population: in 1873, 45 per cent of the county owned less than one acre – 28 per cent in the towns and 17 per cent in rural areas; 44 per cent owned between one and 50 acres, 11 per cent more than 50 acres. Just over a quarter (28 per cent) of Lincolnshire was held in estates of more than 10,000 acres, less than Nottinghamshire (38 per cent) with its 'Dukeries' but more than most other counties.

110

Characteristic of the landlord society was the 'closed' village which belonged entirely or almost entirely to one landlord, resident or non-resident. They were frequent on the Wolds and heathlands and a few existed in the Fens; in Kesteven, nearly half the villages were closed, in Lindsey as a whole about one third, but in Holland they were relatively few.

The landlord of the closed village often restricted the building of new houses and even pulled down empty houses to lessen his liability to the parish poor rate, provided he could draw sufficient extra workers from neighbouring 'open' villages. The Board of Guardians complained

> that the exclusive proprietor (failing to provide the necessary accommodation for the increased population, and not only so, but in some instances indeed pulling down cottages upon his estate, and in many cases suffering them to dilapidate in order to get rid of the poor) had forced that portion of the population which in common fairness belonged to him into the neighbouring market-towns and villages (consisting of small freeholds) . . . and that it had caused such an increase in the poor rates in those localities as to render them almost ruinous.

The labourers moved to the open villages, as James Caird, a Lincolnshire farmer who won a prize in 1851, the Great Exhibition year, with his essay on farming in the county, wrote:

> In some localities, [the labourers] pay very high rents for their cottages, being swept out of close parishes . . . and obliged to compete with each other for the possession of the limited number of cottages which speculators . . . run up in open parishes for their accommodation. They are thus in many cases compelled to live at a great distance from their work, to which it is quite common for them to ride on donkeys a distance of six or seven miles.

They lived in great poverty, according to Cobbett who saw the richness of the land but noted 'it is in the villages that you find the depth of misery', though others have suggested that the Lincolnshire labourer was better off than labourers elsewhere.

Some open villages became very large and earned notoriety as centres of nuisance, 'sink' villages. Morton was contrasted with Sir Gilbert Heathcote's Hacconby nearby:

Pelham's pillar, Cadbourne

> while the property of this large parish continues divided and in so many hands, each individual proprietor will consider himself at liberty to act independently. His example is insensibly imitated by his inferiors who, gradually growing in lawless habits, have no notion of that decent deportment and necessary subordination visible in market towns and villages belong[ing] solely either to some virtuous nobleman or to a resident gentleman.

Places like Kelsey, Coningsby, Wrangle and Binbrook had similar reputations.

The gangs of agricultural labourers which lived in these open villages soon gave their name to groups of criminals: at Morton there was 'frequent house-breaking attended with open and outrageous violence by a gang of masqued thieves who came armed; mischievous acts cruel

111

to both man and beast, kept the public and private mind in continual alarm'. The magistrates transported troublemakers, and the clergy exhorted the adults and educated the young in their public responsibilities, but ineffectually. The county constabulary was created in 1857, gaols like Folkingham (1808) were built, public lunatic asylums replaced private ones like Greatford and Shillingthorpe, and the local militia was developed (the Lincolnshire Regiment was formed in 1881). Landlord, freeholder, substantial tenant farmer and clergy combined in an onslaught on 'peasant culture' on an unprecedented scale – mumming plays, football, bull-baiting and the 'rudeness . . . and unbridled behaviour' of the labouring classes at fair time.

Depression

The growing sense of identity of the agricultural labourer led to the 'Revolt of the Field' of the 1870s. In one sense this agitation reflected the increased security of the labourer, especially when faced with the end of the good times which followed the Crimea War. A series of disasters struck the county – cattle plague in 1866, 'the worst rains on record' in 1879, foot and mouth disease in the 1880s, and through it all the Great Depression of the 1870s-80s. At first it was the landholder who suffered from the poor yields, expensive harvesting and low corn prices. Rents were rebated and arrears (sometimes as high as £2000) written off, since 'never before have the cultivators of the land suffered as much as they have of late from a succession of unfavourable seasons and other causes'. The rent takers lost much of their income; clergy who relied heavily on glebe lost as much as three-quarters of their rents. The result was that 'many old estates have been sold and broken up and are now replaced by an infinite number of small holdings and an incredible number of small freeholds, with no game, no resident proprietors, no large places or estates'.

But in the end it was the labourer who came off worst: 'labourers do begin in some instances to emigrate from the land'. Cheap Irish labour was brought in for seasonal work. When the Great Depression began to bite, the farming community saw that 'many farmers may be reduced to labourers and then be compelled to emigrate when nothing is left to them but poverty and wretchedness'. The labourer, fearful for his job and the tenancy of his tied cottage, became increasingly resentful. Reluctant to break traditional community bonds but emboldened by his allegiance to and training in Primitive Methodism, he began his way towards unionism. A national farmworkers' union was not established until 1906, but the foundations were laid by the strikes and associations, especially in the Fens, between 1872 and 1882.

Industry and towns

There were relatively few manufacturing or extractive industries in Lincolnshire to which the labourer could turn. The coast offered tourism,

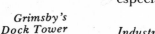

Grimsby's Dock Tower

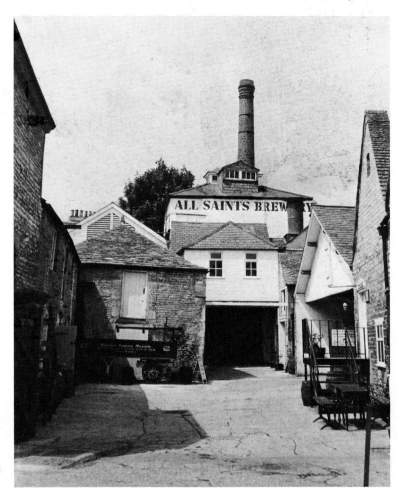

43. All Saints' Brewery, Stamford, one of the many maltings which processed locally-produced barley.

44. An example of estate housing in a 'closed' village (Brocklesby).

45. The 19th century saw the development of several coastal towns as holiday resorts: Cleethorpes Pier.

46. Bourne market place, showing the town hall (1821).

47. Sugar beet factory, Spalding, an indicator of the importance of the land in 20th-century Lincolnshire.

48. A 'Dambuster' bomb preserved at R.A.F. Scampton, commemorating the strikes made from Lincolnshire airfields during the Second World War.

49. Spalding Flower Festival and Parade, 1982.

50. A fly-past over the R.A.F. Cadet College, Cranwell.

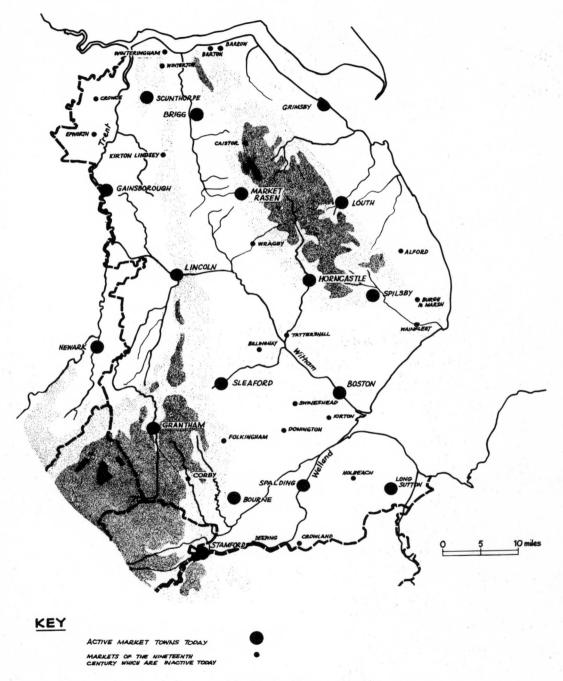

KEY

ACTIVE MARKET TOWNS TODAY

MARKETS OF THE NINETEENTH
CENTURY WHICH ARE INACTIVE TODAY

24. Market Towns.

113

fishing and work in the docks; elsewhere there were stone and ironstone quarries. The village brick and tile works were hit by the slump, and milling, malting and brewing were moving into larger and more mechanised premises in towns like Spalding, Sleaford, Grantham and especially Newark. A good deal remained in the countryside – brewing, crushing seeds for oil, coach building and canvas and sack making in Epworth and elsewhere, and John Parkinson established his unsuccessful factory for crepes and bombazine in the Fens at New Bolingbroke, not in one of the towns. But these all used relatively little labour.

The towns of Lincolnshire had little effect on the surrounding country-side or even on each other as bridgeheads of urban culture. They were more influenced by rural society rather than being centres of influence themselves. Lincoln in 1859 was 'a place which almost stood by itself – isolated as it were in the midst of an agricultural district', and Grimsby's impact was reduced by having within its boundaries 'an insulating layer [of rural parishes] between the borough and the country'.

There were no national centres in Lincolnshire as there had been in the Middle Ages. Instead the network of market towns which grew up in the 17th century served the county well. A few, the coaching towns with their theatres, assembly rooms, inns and fine houses, had become centres for the diffusion of fashion – Lincoln, Stamford, Boston, Grantham and to a lesser extent Spalding and Grimsby; while spa towns were established or attempted at Woodhall Spa (hotel and bath house, 1838-9), Braceborough and Stamford, and from 1799 the coastal resorts advertised to attract visitors for the season. Literary and philosophical societies as at Spalding and Stamford and other features of urban life attracted gentry and clergy to reside in these places.

Turnpike roads and waterways helped the growth of places like Market Deeping, Gainsborough and Louth, while Long Sutton and Brigg grew up on the backs of drainage schemes. The railways for a time fostered markets and fairs and increased the focal role of the town with its newspapers and banks; they also helped new industries to develop and led to the expansion of the coastal resorts. But most towns in the region declined in the later 19th century, along with the rural areas they depended upon. Throughout the county, fairs and markets like Stow Green, Kirton in Holland and Swineshead ('now nearly deserted . . . little business done . . . except in the evening when the principal farmers assemble at the *Griffin Inn*') dwindled. The pull of Hull in the north, Leicester, Nottingham and Newark in the west contributed.

A few places grew. Grantham benefited from the enclosure of the heathlands around and the canal; factories grew up by the canal wharves. When the railway sheds were established (1852), the town changed from an agricultural market and staging post with inns and hotels into an industrial centre and railway junction with heavy and light engineering. Gainsborough built up an extensive carrying trade on the Trent between Nottingham and Hull; its ship building came to outstrip East Stockwith

Brittania Works,
Gainsborough

114

nearby. In the early 19th century, iron foundries and engineering works grew up. The coming of the railways hurt the river-borne trade but growth began again in the 1860s based on mills, maltings and breweries. The great days of Stamford with its coaches to London, York, Leeds, Edinburgh, Leicester and Cambridge, were over, but some brewing and engineering sprang up despite the lack of a main line railway.

The towns serviced the countryside, milling, malting, tanning, processing and supplying fertilisers and machinery; shops, markets and services were the mainstays of their economy. The large-scale industrial growth of Victorian England passed the region by; only one textile mill (Lincoln) was built in the county though the Handley brothers of Sleaford and others set up mills in Newark and other places. Some sacking and linen manufactories, rope works and worsted weaving plants were put up but none grew into a stable industry. Only engineering became significant. Grantham and Lincoln relied on it; Howden's foundries at Boston produced one of the first steam threshing machines (1803), the steam river packet (1827) and the portable steam engine (1839). Marshalls of Gainsborough (founded in 1842) produced new lines of farm engines.

The towns depended on the prosperity of the countryside. Louth with its canal trade based on wool and coal flourished as farming on the Wolds flourished and declined with it. They remained small: in some respects they resembled open villages in their poverty and popular disturbances. Boston, the home of the radical John Wilks, expanded in the early 19th century but declined with the coming of the railways; as elsewhere the town came to be full of 'courts', back yards built up with poor 'hutches', primitive cottages or hovels. Horncastle in an attempt to gain 'an air of respectability' saw a good deal of new building, but the crowded town and annual horse fair were reputed to have led to crime, violence and disease. The popular festivities of the towns, like the bull baiting at Stamford, were rural in character and suppressed by their social superiors.

Customs House, Boston

Lincoln did not differ markedly from this general pattern. Although the county town, it had never become the capital of its region in the way Leicester, York or Nottingham had. It did not even influence the culture of other towns like Louth or Grantham. After the decline in the 16th century which made its name a by-word for 'decay'd towns' in general, the city began to recover from the end of the 17th century, when gentry from the surrounding countryside moved into the town. Population grew, from about 3000 in the 1670s to 5000 in the 1750s and more than 7000 in 1800. The medieval walls were removed, the main roads improved by the turnpike trusts (1756) and New Road was built to ease access to the upper city (1785). The city gained new markets (1736), a race course (moved in 1771 to Carholme), assembly rooms (1757, moved to the upper city in 1774), a hospital (1769) and County Hall in the castle (1776). A coach ran to London, weekly until 1784 and daily from 1791; by 1837 some 30 coaches plied to the capital each week carrying

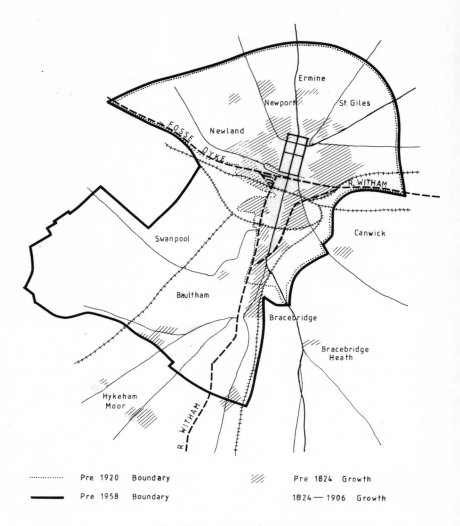

Pre 1920   Boundary   ⁄⁄⁄   Pre 1824   Growth

Pre 1958   Boundary   1824—1906   Growth

25. Modern Lincoln.

All Saints'
Brewery,
Stamford

13,500 passengers each year. Daily services ran to Hull, Rotherham, Nottingham and other places.

In 1741 Richard Ellison of Boultham leased the Fosse Dyke from the city for £175 p.a. and increased the value of the tolls to more than £7000 p.a. From 1762 the Witham was developed and a steam packet ran regularly to Boston from 1826. The enclosure of the heathlands north and south of Lincoln led to increased affluence in the region, and an expansion of the town's marketing services and industrial activities. Tanneries, mills and maltings grew up along the Witham and round Brayford Pool. It remained the centre of the county's religious and secular life. At first smaller than Boston, its growth was sluggish until the railways boosted its industrial life and gave a new focus to the town's factories. Links with Nottingham (1846), Peterborough and London (1848), Grantham (1867), Sheffield, and other centres made it a focal

116

point; the network was completed by 1896. As early as 1846 the railways bought up the Fosse and Witham Navigations.

The population of the city doubled twice, from 7000 (1800) to 13,800 (1840) and to nearly 27,000 (1870). Most of the new residents were housed in the existing town and in the bottom of the Gap, but Bracebridge Heath on the southern slope sprang up from 1841. The owners of Boultham and Canwick bordering on the city were reluctant to release land for building; space was sought in Boultham (from 1876), Bracebridge (1870s) and North Hykeham (from 1900). In the city, Newland and Monks Road were laid out after an Act of 1860 freed two areas of commons, but expansion to east and west was limited. The upper city remained distinct; the only industry there was a short-lived rope industry, and until 1835 the Bail was administratively separate from the rest of Lincoln.

'The increase in the population of the city of Lincoln is mainly attributable to the extension of the Iron manufactures', wrote the 1871 census officers; 18 per cent of the working population was engaged in Lincoln's iron-working industries which grew to international significance. Clayton and Shuttleworth, founded in 1842, employed 1300 people. Burton and Proctor (later Rustons) built their Sheaf Works at Stamp Lock, where they produced and exported threshing machines and steam engines. Although there was some flour milling (Charles Seeley) and some chemical plants, by the early 20th century Lincoln was largely a one-industry town. Most of the new factories and engineering sheds grew up near the railway stations and marshalling yards.

Lincoln outstripped Boston by the mid-Victorian period, but it was still not the largest town in the region; that role was now occupied by Grimsby which became one of the most important fishing ports in the country, especially after the development of the steam trawler in the 1880s. As the town grew, the neighbouring resort of Cleethorpes came to be less attractive to the genteel visitor, and from 1863 when Cleethorpes and Grimsby were linked by railway, it became a holiday centre for the industrial towns of the north. Skegness was promoted jointly by Lord Scarbrough and the railway companies after the village had been linked to the Boston-Grimsby line in 1873. It too became a resort, its pier (1881) and gardens laid out after the building of the sea wall in 1878. Other resorts on the coast followed, so that by 1903 the area had become 'the great summer playground of the working-classes in Nottinghamshire, Derbyshire and Leicestershire, besides drawing in many from Yorkshire and even Lancashire . . . conveyed by the . . . northern railways in express excursion trains, every day through the summer, at fares for which, south of London, one could hardly get to the suburbs'.

Industrial growth took place in some newer centres. Iron ore was extracted at Frodingham from the 1860s and in south-west Kesteven, and Scunthorpe iron works developed from 1875, for a time one of the largest producers of steel in England. Rowland Winn of Appleby

'Steam Navvy' excavating machine

117

promoted railway links with Sheffield in the 1860s. But the growth of Scunthorpe, Grimsby and Skegness meant the decline of the older centres like Stamford and Boston, and the death of smaller markets like Folkingham and Wragby.

Manor Farm, Somersby

XIV The Twentieth Century

Lincolnshire today is one vast food factory for the nation. But recovery from the Depression of the 1870s was slow. Holland benefited first: in 1906 the Fens were 'a sunny oasis' in an otherwise bleak picture. Cheap grains from America led to a reduction in the amount of land under arable, and land prices fell; the church in Lincolnshire began to sell its glebe. Small holdings were established, especially around the Wash following the Small Holdings Act of 1908. During World War I farming was for a short time a matter of national concern, but when the war was over, price guarantees were withdrawn (1921), Canadian corn flooded in and prices and land values fell again: 'the great betrayal', it was called. In the recession which followed, farmers turned first to new arable crops, then to stock, chickens and bullocks and finally back to arable.

Early tank made at Lincoln

As the 19th-century gangs became increasingly a thing of the past, the labourer found himself working in the fields on his own. Women joined the labour force during the war, but as farmers turned to mixed farming and market gardens, the use of labour was cut: Lincolnshire with one of the largest hired forces in the country suffered severely. With shooting restricted and myxomatosis having 'done poor folk out of a dinner', many labourers only had casual employment. The brief but bitter strike of the National Union of Agricultural Workers (1923) solved neither of the problems which pressed on the labourer, the tied cottage and the deference the farmer required and inevitably got.

There was little support in Lincolnshire for the General Strike of 1926; indeed volunteers were recruited and mobilised in Lincoln 'to maintain supplies'. But the National Government of 1931 with its policy of 'Protection without interference' took agriculture more seriously. The Milk Marketing Board was set up in 1933-5, and the Potato and Egg Boards followed, particularly important for Lincolnshire with its mixed farming.

World War II saw some bombing in Scunthorpe, Grimsby and elsewhere, evacuees from the Midlands and the north, and American troops and German prisoners of war. 'Home food production' was the theme of the Agricultural Executive Committee of which there was a branch in every county. Fuel, fertilisers and other supplies were controlled and grants for ploughing grassland and other improvements made available. Marginal land was pressed into service for the first time in many years, and many Lincolnshire farms and villages were rebuilt at this time; vehicles like the jeep, designed for the army, were used on the farms.

Protection continued after the war with the Agriculture Act (1947); the annual price review led to jibes of 'feather-bedded farmers'. Output grew very little between 1920 and 1950, but from 1950 to 1980 it rose by nearly 100 per cent. The policy agreed between the National Farmers Union and the Labour government was continued under the tories. But the cost of protection was regulation – of acreages ploughed, of stock, of pest control (such as foot and mouth slaughter policies) together with soaring land prices. As all crops were seen to be profitable, the range grown in Lincolnshire widened. Intensive farming (pigs and hens) led to a demand for small plots of land, and local authorities and private associations laid out small holdings, as at Eastville, especially after the wars.

In the 1960s the farmers fought the proposal to join the EEC but accepted it in 1972. As livestock suffered and cereals gained, Lincolnshire with more than 60 per cent arable land profited. The speed of 'improvements' (like the removal of hedges and the creation of larger fields for ploughing) grew. New machinery was introduced first in the dairy, then in the field – binder, combines in the 1930s and others; corn driers are both a means to and symbol of the wealth of the modern Lincolnshire farmer. The application of chemicals, now by aerial spraying, has led to the constant use of the land without rest. New strains have been produced by research, and yields per acre increased, as have milk yields. The use of labour has continued to fall. In 1926 the county had some 40,000 agricultural workers, by 1982 less than 10,000; in Lindsey the number of farmworkers fell from 15,500 (1959) to 8300 (1969). Seasonal labour (for example for the beet harvest) comes more from outside than from the towns and villages of the county.

The conversion of mixed farming back to arable begun in the late 19th century continued. Between 1925 and 1975, wheat acreages doubled, barley and beet trebled. Less land is occupied by potatoes, fruit and cattle, and sheep now utilise less than half the land they formerly grazed. In the 1960s, Lindsey and Kesteven produced barley, wheat and rotation grass; in the Fens where most grass is ley grass in rotation with wheat or barley, sugar beet or potatoes, the main crops were wheat, potatoes, barley and fruit. New crops have been introduced – sugar, peas, onions, cabbages, carrots, bulbs in the Fens and rape on the heaths. Market gardens and direct selling to the passer by are characteristic of parts of the county.

Some of this produce is processed locally: the sugar factories at Brigg, Bardney and Spalding are amongst the largest in the country. Newark, Peterborough and King's Lynn process beet from Lincolnshire. Until 1948 much of the beet went by water, until the 1960s by rail; now it goes by lorry. Food processing, canning, freezing and the making of potato crisps, is a major industry in the Sutton area and around Grimsby (Ross, Bird's Eye, Findus, Salvesen and Smiths).

Cement is extracted at South Ferriby, Kirton in Lindsey and else-

Sloop

where, iron ore until recently in the Scunthorpe area and south of Grantham; for a time the county produced nearly twice as much low grade ore as any other region. The lower Trent valley has developed as one of the largest electricity producing regions in Europe.

By 1914 Lincoln was at the peak of its industrial career. Most of its workers were engaged in munitions and railway engineering; the first tanks and some of the first aircraft were built in the town. New suburbs grew up in St Giles and Boultham (incorporated into the city in 1920), and Ruston and Hornsby laid out a 'garden suburb' in Swanpool. After the war came a slump; from 66,000 (1921) Lincoln grew to only 69,000 (1951). In 1933-4, 8000 men were recorded as unemployed, and attempts were made to diversify the town's economy. World War II ended the slump and the town grew to 76,600 (1981). Apart from service occupations (the largest group), the city is still dependent on engineering, concentrated in the south east; the inner road over Pelham Bridge (1961) gave recognition to the new heart of Lincoln.

The north is the industrialised region of Lincolnshire. Scunthorpe, where the manufacture of steel began in the 1890s, threatened at one stage to become 'a second Middlesborough'. From a population of 1,700 (1864), it grew to 26,000 (1918) and to 69,900 in 1965; since then it has fallen to 66,600 (1981). New housing sprang up at New Frodingham and New Brumby. Grimsby, a general port with much coal trade, is still one of the country's most important fishing centres, whether viewed in terms of the size of fleet, value of catch or numbers of fishermen. Immingham port, built 1906-12, and Killingholme oil terminal and refinery are part of the Humberside industrial development; exports of iron and steel, coal and chemicals are matched by imports of wood, oil and foodstuffs. Chemical works as at Flixborough (scene of a disaster in 1974) have been developed. The region has since 1974 been transferred into a new county of Humberside, and the development of new transport systems with crossings of the Trent and Humber has helped to create new community bonds and new industrial opportunities.

Outside Humberside, Lincolnshire industries are still connected with agriculture. Diesel pumps were installed in the drainage areas (as at Black Sluice 1946) in place of steam; they are now being replaced with electric pumps. Hornsby of Grantham produced the first farm tractor (1896), but horses continued to be the norm on Lincolnshire farms until after World War II. Rustons of Lincoln and Hornsby of Grantham merged and their factories were rationalised.

The towns still depend on agriculture. The docks at Boston import timber and export agricultural produce. Gainsborough has engineering (Marshalls' tractors), Louth a packaging industry and Spalding the sugar and bulb industries. But the markets have continued to decline. Railway lines were built on the coast (1910-12) and across the Fens (1913), but freight traffic returned to the roads. This, and the removal of stock markets from town centres to permanent peripheral sites, have contributed to the decline of fairs and markets, until today only 14

Herbert Ingram, journalist and M.P. for Boston

121

centres survive. At Horncastle the largest horse fair in England ceased in 1948, and with it the number of inns and public houses fell from over 60 to 13; the town still repairs farmers' tools, supplies their necessities and processes their produce, but many who live in Horncastle now work in Lincoln or elsewhere.

Commuters have saved the lives of many villages; the Deepings, for example, house some of the working population of Peterborough. The countryside has been transformed over the last 50 years. The presence of large numbers of cars and new housing are the most visible signs of this, but with these have come the re-organisation of education (Kesteven extended secondary education to all its pupils when it opened three new schools at Billingborough, Billinghay and Corby in 1964, doing away with the last of its all age schools), the decline in numbers of the rural clergy (who may now serve as many as seven parishes) and increasing non-residence of both teacher and incumbent, but at the same time a spectacular increase in voluntary societies and organisations. The coast attracts the retired and holiday maker; Butlin opened the first holiday camp in the country at Ingoldmells in 1936, while at Skegness three-quarters of a million holiday makers were recorded before the First World War. Holiday camps and caravan parks sprang up, especially at Cleethorpes, Mablethorpe and Skegness. Lindsey County Council bought large stretches of the coast under an Act of 1932.

The land is still Lincolnshire's greatest asset. One of its contributions to the war effort of this century was the provision of many and large airfields from as early as 1912, of which Scampton, Coningsby and especially the R.A.F. College at Cranwell are permanent reminders. But it is food production which has dominated the county; indeed it can be said of Lincolnshire that it is one of England's most highly industrialised counties – the industry being agriculture.

Alfred,
Lord Tennyson,
born at
Somersby

Select Bibliography

The History of Lincolnshire Committee, in 1965, started to publish a series of 12 volumes on the ancient county; so far eight volumes have appeared and the remaining four are in hand. This is the fullest account of Lincolnshire's past to date. Only one volume of the projected Victoria County History for Lincolnshire has appeared, but it is invaluable. The only general surveys of the county's history published within recent years are C. Brears, *A Short History of Lincolnshire* (1927) and M.W. Barley's valuable book, *Lincolnshire and the Fens* (1952). M. Lloyd's *Lincolnshire: a portrait* (1983) is a topographical guide but it contains much original material drawn mainly from the wide range of sources of the Lincolnshire Archives Office. Also of general interest are the earlier topographical and architectural guidebooks, Arthur Mee's *Lincolnshire* (revised edition, ed. F.T. Baker, 1970) and N. Pevsner and J. Harris, *The Buildings of England: Lincolnshire* (1964: revised edition is in hand). Joan Varley's useful little book, *The Parts of Kesteven, studies in law and local government* (1974) covers a wide range of topics from the Domesday period down to 1974. *See also* Hill's volumes on Lincoln, cited below.

On some of the topics discussed in this book, there is little easily available. The following books and articles, however, are the most important works to be consulted. They must be taken together with the three most important sources of Lincolnshire's history: the annual volumes published by the Lincoln Record Society, especially the introductions to each volume; the articles and papers in the *Reports of the Lincolnshire Archaeological and Architectural Society* (down to 1964; from 1850 to 1937 these papers were included in the *Reports and Papers of the Associated Architectural Societies*); and thirdly the journal of what is now the Society for Lincolnshire History and Archaeology which has appeared under various titles – *The Lincolnshire Historian* (1948-1964) and *Lincolnshire History and Archaeology* from 1966, when the old Lincolnshire Local History Society joined with the even older Archaeological and Architectural Society.

An early attempt at a county historical journal, the *Lincoln Magazine* published by the diocese of Lincoln, contains much which is still of value. The *East Midland Geographer* and the *Bulletin of Local History, East Midlands Region*, both published by the University of Nottingham, often contain useful articles on Lincolnshire's history; more occasional papers appear in *Midland History* (Birmingham University) and in the *Journal of Local and Regional History* (Humberside Institute of Higher Education). Also to be examined are *Lincolnshire Notes and Queries* (1888-1936) and the annual reports of the Lincolnshire Archives Office.

Geography
V. Wilson, *British Regional Geology, East Yorkshire and Lincolnshire*, 2nd edn. by P.E. Kent, H.M.S.O., 1980; H.H. Swinnerton and P.E. Kent, *The Geology of Lincolnshire*, 2nd edn., 1976; K.C. Edwards, ed., *Nottingham and its region*, 1966 (which contains many geographical and historical essays on Lincolnshire).

Archaeology
C.W. Phillips, 'The Present State of Archaeology in Lincolnshire', *Archaeological Journal*, vols. XC and XCI, 1933, 1934; F.T. Baker, *Roman Lincoln*, 1938; J. May, *Prehistoric Lincolnshire* (History of Lincolnshire vol.1), 1976; J.B. Whitwell, *Roman Lincolnshire* (History of Lincolnshire, vol.2), 1970.

The Settlements
K. Cameron, *Scandinavian settlement in the territory of the Five Boroughs*, 1965; K.C. Cameron, ed., *Place-name Evidence for the Anglo-Saxon Invasion and Scandinavian Settlements*, (English Place-Name Society), 1975; C. Phythian-Adams, 'The Emergence of Rutland and the Making of the Realm', *Rutland Record*, 1980. Just published is Pauline Stafford's important *East Midlands in the Early Middle Ages*, 1985.

Domesday Lincolnshire
H.C. Darby, *The Domesday Geography of Eastern England*, 1952.

Lincolnshire Monasteries and Churches
D. Knowles and R.N. Hadcock, *Medieval Religious Houses, England and Wales*, 1953; *Victoria County History: Lincolnshire*, vol.2, 1906 (this is the only volume to be published – it contains essays on Lincolnshire's political and social history as well as accounts of the Lincolnshire monasteries); N. Pevsner and J. Harris, *The Buildings of England: Lincolnshire*, 1964; D.M. Owen, *Church and Society in Medieval Lincolnshire* (History of Lincolnshire, vol.5), 1971.

Medieval Lincolnshire

E. Carus Wilson, 'The Medieval Trade of the Ports of the Wash', *Medieval Archaeology*, vols. 6, 7, 1962-3; W.I. Haward, 'The Trade of Boston in the Fifteenth Century', *Reports of Associated Architectural Societies*, vol.XLI, 1933; H.C. Darby, *Historical Geography of England before 1800*, 1963 (several papers – these essays cover many other topics, from prehistory to turnpike roads); H.E. Hallam, *Settlement and Society*, 1965 (a study of the Lincolnshire Fens in the 13th century).

Tudor and Stuart Lincolnshire

G. Hodgett, *Tudor Lincolnshire* (History of Lincolnshire, vol.6), 1975; C. Holmes, *Seventeenth Century Lincolnshire* (History of Lincolnshire, vol.7), 1980; E. Mansell Sympson, 'Lincolnshire and the Civil War', *Memorials of Old Lincolnshire*, 1911; A.C. Wood, *Nottinghamshire in the Civil Wars*, 1937; A.C. Wood, 'Colonel Sir Edward Rossiter', *Reports of Associated Architectural Societies*, vol.XLI, 1933.

The Fens

W.H. Wheeler, *A History of the Fens of South Lincolnshire*, 1896; H.C. Darby, *The Medieval Fenland*, 1940; H.C. Darby, *The Changing Fenland*, 1983; K. Lindley, *Fenland Riots and the English Revolution*, 1982.

Agricultural Changes

J. Thirsk, *English Peasant Farming*, 1957 (a history of Lincolnshire farming, 1600-1870); D. Grigg, *The Agricultural Revolution in South Lincolnshire*, 1966; J. Thirsk, *Fenland Farming in the Sixteenth Century*, 1953; T.W. Beastall, *The Agricultural Revolution in Lincolnshire*, (History of Lincolnshire, vol.8), 1978. *See also* J. Thirsk, 'The Isle of Axholme before Vermuyden', *Agricultural History Review*, vol.1, 1953; *Read's History of the Isle of Axholme*, 1858, reprinted 1980; R.C. Russell, *The 'Revolt of the Field' in Lincolnshire*, 1956; A. Young, *General View of the Agriculture of the County of Lincolnshire*, 1813, reprinted 1970. There are many local studies of enclosure, especially the booklets written by Rex C. Russell, such as *The Enclosure of Barton on Humber*, 1968.

Religious History

V.H.H. Green, *John Wesley*, 1964 (the best general work produced recently, with extensive bibliographies); J. Obelkevich, *Religion and Rural Society, South Lindsey 1825-1875*, 1976; R.W. Ambler, ed., *Lincolnshire Returns of the Census of Religious Worship, 1851* (Lincoln Record Society, vol.72), 1979.

Turnpikes, Canals and Railways

C. Hadfield, *The Canals of the East Midlands*, 1966; N. Wright, *Lincolnshire Towns and Industry, 1700-1914* (History of Lincolnshire, vol.11), 1982; C. Brears, *Lincolnshire in the Seventeenth and Eighteenth Centuries*, 1940; R.E. Pearson, 'Railways in Relation to Resort Development in East Lincolnshire', *East Midland Geographer*, December 1966; D.M. Smith, *The Industrial Architecture of the East Midlands*, 1965; J.G. Ruddock and R.E. Pearson, *Railway History of Lincoln*, 1974.

Lincoln

Sir Francis Hill's series on the city is the main achievement of recent years: *Medieval Lincoln*, 1948; *Tudor and Stuart Lincoln*, 1956; *Georgian Lincoln*, 1966; and *Victorian Lincoln*, 1974. In each case these volumes cover a much wider field than the history of Lincoln; they contain much of value on the history of the county.

Nineteenth Century

R.J. Olney, *Lincolnshire Politics 1832-1885*, 1973; R.J. Olney, *Rural Society and County Government in Nineteenth Century Lincolnshire* (History of Lincolnshire, vol.10), 1979; D.I.A. Steel, *A Lincolnshire Village*, 1979.

Lincolnshire Towns

There are a number of local studies. Among the most useful are: E. Gillett, *History of Grimsby*, 1970; I. Beckwith, *The Making of Modern Gainsborough* (a series of booklets on that town's history); publications of the history of Boston project, 1970-78; A. Rogers, *The Book of Stamford*, 1983; A. Rogers, ed., *The Making of Stamford*, 1965; G.H. Martin, *The Royal Charters of Grantham*, 1963; F. Baker, *The Story of Cleethorpes*, 1953; F. Henthorn, *History of Brigg Grammar School*, 1959. *See also* R.C. Russell, *History of Schools and Education in Lindsey, 1800-1901* (a series of booklets begun in 1965 and still in progress, published by the Lindsey County Council); M. Honeybone, *The Book of Grantham*, 1980; D. Kaye, *The Book of Grimsby*, 1981; D.N. Robinson, *The Book of Louth*, 1979; D.N. Robinson, *The Book of the Lincolnshire Seaside, 1981*.

Index

126